Praise

'In business and life, storms are inevitable. *Be More Buffalo* offers powerful, actionable frameworks to not just survive, but thrive – by facing them head-on. I highly recommend this book!'

— **Andrea Waltz**, co-author, *Go for No!*

'Jamie has written a book that every business owner should keep within arm's reach. It's part story, part playbook, and entirely inspiring. The clarity and encouragement that shines through in *Be More Buffalo* has transformed the way I approach networking. This book will help you face your own storms with confidence.'

— **Chris Griffiths**, Owner Director, Voicon

'I've adapted the concept of "being more buffalo" into the whole of my business strategy and the results have been staggering for our business. I've always been an action taker but this takes it to a whole new level. I can't wait to share this book with all of my business contacts and help them to "be more buffalo".'

— **Paul McGowan**, Managing Director, How? Financial Review

'This isn't just a business book, it's a guide to changing how you move through challenges. As Jamie so powerfully shows through Sophie's journey, "the longer you avoid the storm, the longer it controls you". The practical tools, the clear action steps, and the caring tone will make you want to fold page corners, make notes in the margin, and return to whenever life starts to feel reactive instead of intentional.

'*Be More Buffalo* is not just about building a business, it's about building resilience, purpose, and the courage to move forward "one decision at a time". *Be More Buffalo* transforms conversations, unlocks momentum, and gives people a way to step into their next chapter with clarity and confidence.'

— **Elliot Kay**, CEO, The Speaker Awards and Summit

'This book encapsulates the power of the community – it tells a story that business owners can relate to and use to enhance the power of our experience and business friendships. It is rare to find a business book that gives such a powerful blueprint to challenge you about how you want to be seen and work.

'I've read hundreds of business books and this is one of the few that made me want to take action immediately – and showed how best to do it. Congratulations Jamie. This feels like the beginning of a truly impactful series of guides to doing business. Thank you so much for sharing.'

— **Edward Ferris**, investor and NED,
Chair Hip Pop

'*Be More Buffalo* is a refreshing and practical guide to the power of authentic networking and referrals. Jamie has captured the essence of building meaningful connections that create lasting value, both personally and professionally. This book is not just about strategies, but about cultivating the mindset and generosity that transform contacts into trusted relationships. A must-read for anyone who believes that success is built through people helping people.'

— **Gautam Ganglani**, CEO, Right Selection
Global Thought Leadership

'I was in tears by the end of the first chapter, as I recognised my own familiar struggles from the past. Although I'm now thriving in business, I love to keep *Be More Buffalo* by my side as a constant reminder and a living, working document. So much more than a book, it's a manifesto for how to do networking and how to grow your business.'

— **Ailsa Stinson**, CEO, B is for Brand

BE MORE
Charge ahead in business and life
BUFFALO

JAMIE STEWART
with GILLIAN SCHOFIELD

Rethink

First published in Great Britain in 2025
by Rethink Press (www.rethinkpress.com)

Contents

Introduction: Sophie In The Storm

Sophie sat curled on the sofa, her laptop balanced on one knee, a half-finished mug of Yorkshire Tea on the armrest. Her inbox was open, and one subject line held her attention: 'Ending our retainer'. With a sinking stomach, she clicked into the email again, even though she had already read it. Twice. 'Thanks for everything you've done for us. The business is changing direction and we're bringing design in-house.' It was polite. Professional. Final.

That retainer had paid half her bills for the past year. This was the second major client in two weeks to quietly step away. It wasn't personal, but it still hit hard. Fighting the rising worry, she clicked into another tab and stared at a half-written post she'd been fighting with all week. She just didn't have the nerve to finish and publish.

> Need a designer?

She deleted the line and closed the tab. Too vague, too desperate and not really her.

Her phone buzzed beside her. It was a message from Katie Turner, a friend Sophie had met just after she started the business a couple of years earlier.

> Saw this and thought of you, give it a watch, Sophie.

Keen for a distraction, Sophie tapped the YouTube link in the message. The screen filled with a sweep of golden grass under a heavy sky. A herd of buffalo moved slowly across a ridge, their dark shapes almost blending into the land. In the distance, storm clouds were gathering, thick and rolling, the kind that seem to swallow the horizon.

The camera cut closer. A low rumble of thunder rolled through the speakers. The narrator explained that while most animals turn and run from an oncoming storm, buffalo do the opposite. Sophie watched as the herd paused, their heads lifting as if they'd caught a scent on the wind. The first drops of rain fell. A flash lit the screen, followed by a crack of lightning.

Then, as the storm bore down, the buffalo turned towards it. They lowered their heads and began to move, slowly at first, then breaking into a charge, muscles heaving, pounding straight into the sheets of rain. The voiceover said that by facing the storm, buffalo move through it faster, reaching clear skies sooner.

Sophie paused the video. The house was still and quiet; amazingly, the teens were already asleep. The kitchen was still a mess from the chaos of teatime – but none of that mattered right now. Inspired by what she'd heard, Sophie picked up her notebook and wrote:

> **Most people try to avoid the storm. I've been doing that too. Maybe it's time to face it.**

She didn't know what that would involve – not yet – but she did know what avoidance had already cost her: time, confidence, money, energy. Maybe the storm itself wasn't the real problem. Maybe it was the running.

• • •

This book follows Sophie's journey as she begins to choose differently, not through dramatic change, but by thinking more clearly, acting more deliberately and facing the things she's been avoiding. You'll see her question habits she once relied on and learn to work with more purpose and less pressure. You'll walk by her side as she lets go of fear and procrastination and begins to build a solid and sustainable business. Along the way, you'll have the opportunity to do the same by working through the questions at the end of each chapter. If you've been drifting, juggling too much or quietly wondering if there's a better way to run your business, this book is for you.

This isn't a book you just read and pop on a shelf. It's a book in which to fold pages, highlight and write – all of that will help you remember the lessons and make them stick. You can read it all in one go or take it a chapter at a time. There's no right or wrong, but if you want to see real results, the most important part is this: do the action steps. You can complete these as you go, or read the whole book and then come back to them and work through them properly. Don't just nod along and move on, never to return.

I'll bet you've read books on business improvement before, and nothing changed as a result. This time, I want you to see progress. To feel the change and build momentum. To take what's in here and use it. That will take a new approach: a notebook beside you, time set aside and a decision to stop waiting and start moving.

Get ready to complete the small actions, be honest in your reflection, and create better habits, one decision at a time. Sophie's not out of the storm yet, but she's about to face it and start seeing results. Maybe you will, too.

ONE

Driftwood Valley

Sophie had opened the same file three times and still hadn't done anything with it. Her coffee had gone cold. Again.

She stared at the screen, trying to muster some enthusiasm about the mood board she was supposed to finalise. The deadline wasn't for another two days, but she had used to be the kind of person who delivered things early, not just on time. Now everything seemed to take twice the effort. She switched tabs to check her email. Nothing new.

That small voice in the back of her mind whispered what she already knew. This wasn't about the work. The client was fine, the brief was clear, but she was tired of solving other people's brand problems when her own felt like a blur.

Stuck in the depths of procrastination, she reached for an old notebook and flipped back through the pages: notes from client calls and strategy outlines, scribbled budgets. Then she noticed a tired affirmation she'd written one night after a webinar:

I am building something meaningful.

Was she? The business wasn't new anymore, yet it still felt fragile. Two years in, and the whole thing still relied on her showing up every week, wearing all the hats, juggling the marketing and admin along with every client, every project deliverable and every revision round.

No team. No buffer. No real plan. Just talent, experience and the occasional referral from someone she'd worked with years ago. This wasn't what she'd pictured when she left the agency. She had wanted space, freedom and more time with her kids. Something less pressured and more enjoyable.

At first, she got it. That first year had felt like a breath of fresh air. No meetings about meetings. No navigating egos. Just her, the clients and the work.

But now? She felt like driftwood. Floating along with no real direction. More reactive than proactive. A business in name but not in structure and always one late payment from panic.

She picked up her phone and checked her calendar. Two discovery calls this week. One client was already looking shaky from the budget, and the other hadn't replied to her confirmation message. This wasn't sustainable. She knew it, but she also didn't know what else to do.

She wasn't afraid of hard work – she'd built her whole career on being the reliable one, the fixer, the one who could step in and sort it – but this was different. It wasn't about working harder. It was about holding too much, too often, with no end in sight.

Sophie closed her laptop. Taking a breath, she reached for her journal and wrote:

> What do I want that I'm not giving myself permission to ask for?

There was a long pause before she wrote anything else while she dug deep, beyond the 'shoulds' into her true desires.

> A proper business. Not living project to project. Not just me.

She didn't know what that looked like yet, but writing it down helped. It felt like the first honest thing she'd admitted to herself in months. She sat back in her chair, feeling the stillness of the quiet room as she reflected. Time to stop pretending and get brutally honest. The storm hadn't hit yet, but she could feel the weather changing.

The phone rang, jolting her from her thoughts. She glanced at the screen, expecting it to be a client or another sales call. Instead, she saw the friend who'd sent the YouTube video about buffalo.

Katie Turner.

Sophie let the phone ring once more, then answered. 'Hi,' she said, surprised by how tired she sounded.

'Hi Sophie,' Katie replied. 'Just thought I'd check in. No reason. Just...how are you?'

Sophie hesitated. The usual response, 'Yeah, I'm great thanks,' sat on the tip of her tongue, but something in Katie's voice, or maybe just the timing, cut through her usual filter. 'I'm not great, actually,' Sophie said. 'It's been rough.'

There was a pause. Katie didn't rush to fill the space. She just waited.

Sophie surprised herself again. 'I've just lost two big clients. I'm staring at proposals I can't finish. I'm undercharging, overworking and starting to think I've built a job, not a business. And if one more person says it's just a phase, I might scream.'

Another pause. Then Katie said, 'Want to meet up? That place on the corner still serves proper Yorkshire Tea – you know, your favourite.'

Something heavy in Sophie lifted slightly. 'Thursday at 9.30am?'

'Thursday is perfect.'

They said their goodbyes. Sophie set the phone down, leaned back and stared at the ceiling. She hadn't planned to say any of that, but now it was out, she felt a little lighter. Nothing had really changed, she was still facing the storm, but she was no longer holding it all in.

Something had started to shift. Just quietly and ever so slightly. The kind of shift you notice more in hindsight than in the moment. Thursday couldn't come soon enough.

•••

They met at the little café near the park; it had mismatched chairs and good tea. Katie was already there when Sophie arrived, sitting with a notebook open and a battered paperback face down beside it. 'Strong, like builders tea?' Katie asked, pointing to a steaming-hot mug.

Sophie smiled. 'You remembered.'

'I remember the important things.'

The conversation flowed easily. Katie never pushed or asked what was wrong. They talked about their weeks – Katie's son's latest school project and Sophie's kids' sibling squabbles. Then, when Sophie felt settled, Katie looked at her directly. 'How's it really going?'

Sophie hesitated, then puffed a breath out through pursed lips. 'I feel stuck. I've built something, but it's just…me. And I keep telling myself I want freedom, but what I've really done is create a job I can't escape. It's all so reactive. Like I'm always waiting for clients to decide whether I have a business next month.'

Katie nodded. 'That was me. For longer than I care to admit.'

Sophie looked up at her. 'What changed?'

Katie tapped the book beside her. 'This helped. But not just reading it, actually *doing* it.'

Sophie turned the cover over: *Be More Buffalo*. 'Let me guess,' she said. 'Facing storms?'

Katie smiled. 'Exactly. It's about how most people avoid the hard stuff. But buffalo don't. When a storm's coming, cows run away. They try to outrun the pain, but the storm just hangs over them. Buffalo turn to face it. And when the storm gets close, they charge through it. They get out the other side faster.'

Sophie raised an eyebrow. 'And you read that and just… stopped running?'

Katie laughed. 'Not overnight. But it gave me something to work with. There's a framework in there. It's not the usual kind of fluff, but it's not complex either. It's practical actions. It sort of guides you through.'

Sophie picked up the book. It was certainly well used. Dog-eared pages, notes stuffed into pages and sentences underlined throughout.

'I've brought another copy for you,' Katie said. 'Take this new one. And I got a notebook for you to go with it.'

Sophie hesitated, taken aback by the selfless gesture. 'Are you sure?'

'I want you to have it, Sophie. I know what it's like to feel so bogged down you just don't know which way to turn. Read it. But more importantly, use it. Write in it, mark pages and do the actions. Make it yours just like I have, and I promise you'll start to move forward.'

Sophie held it for a moment and wondered if such a small book could really make that much difference. Then she tucked the book and the notebook into her bag and resolved to give it her all. 'Alright,' she said. 'Let's see what the buffalo do.'

Action steps: Spot the storm

This chapter is about recognition. About naming what you've been carrying and admitting when something needs to change. Use the steps below to help you identify areas for development.

1. Write it down

What storm have you been avoiding facing? It might be a money issue, a lack of direction or something more personal. Get specific.

2. Ask yourself

Reflect on these questions:

- What is this costing me, emotionally or financially, to avoid?
- What would change if I stopped dodging it?

3. Make one decision

It doesn't need to fix everything; just make it clear. For example, a commitment to speak up, change your offer or start something that's yours.

4. Start your notebook

Keep it beside you as you read this book. Use it to capture your reflections, decisions and progress.

5. Say it out loud or share it with someone

Naming your storm out loud makes it more real. Share it with a trusted friend or mentor. You don't need to go it alone.

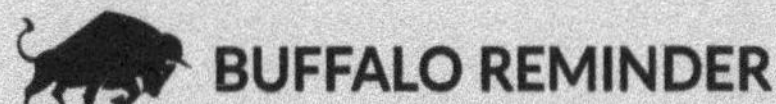

BUFFALO REMINDER

You can't move forward if you won't face what's in front of you.

The longer you avoid the storm, the longer it controls you.

Name it. Map it. Take one step.

The buffalo don't wait for perfect conditions. They face it together. So can you.

To access extra resources, scan the QR code below, or go to www.bemorebuffalo.com.

TWO

Clouds on The Horizon

Sophie stared at the notebook. She'd popped both books on her desk yesterday after the café, but she had retrieved the reading book in the evening and curled up on the sofa to dive into Chapter One. When she reached the reflection questions, she'd closed the book and popped Netflix on to unwind. The notebook had remained where she left it. Untouched.

Now, as she finished up her work for the day, the notebook was niggling at her. She didn't want to admit it, but part of her was afraid to open it. Afraid of what she might write. Afraid her thoughts and answers would only confirm what she already suspected: that the business she'd built needed more than a tidy update. It needed direction, decisions and action.

She ran a hand through her hair, flipped the cover open. A warm and gentle reminder to push through and be honest greeted her on the first page.

'1. Spot the Storm.'

Then in Katie's handwriting:

> Write down what you're avoiding. Then what it's costing you.

Sophie picked up her pen. This time, she didn't hesitate.

> *I'm avoiding:*
>
> *– Raising my rates*
>
> *– Ending relationships with clients who drain me*
>
> *– Putting myself forward as a brand strategist, not just a designer*
>
> *– Hiring help*
>
> *– Being visible*

She paused. Took a breath. Then kept going.

> *What is it costing me?*
>
> *– Time I can't get back*
>
> *– Confidence*

- Money
- Focus
- Pride in my work
- The chance to build something that actually works… that I'm proud of

She sat back and blew out a long breath. It wasn't anything major, but it was from the heart.

Her phone buzzed with a voice note from Katie.

> *You're going to feel some resistance this week. That's normal. Fear always shows up after clarity. But I want you to remember this. Fear is NOT the enemy, Sophie. It's information. It tells you what matters. What's at stake. And where you need to be aiming. Don't fight it, just notice it. Then act anyway. Small steps, that's all.*

Sophie replayed the message. Twice. She wasn't new to fear. She'd just got good at avoiding it. Keeping busy and reactive meant she could always convince herself the timing wasn't right – but maybe this time, she could do it differently.

She turned to a fresh page in the notebook. At the top, she wrote:

Fear list

She drew two columns. She added a few more lines – slowly, giving space and allowing thoughts she'd buried to resurface.

What I'm Afraid of	What I Can Do Anyway
If I raise my rates, I'll lose the client	Talk to one client and trial a new price
Sounding arrogant or salesy in my posts	Write a helpful tips post
If I don't overdeliver, clients won't come back	Set clearer boundaries in the next project

Then she did one small thing. She opened her inbox and tapped out a short email to a client. It wasn't an upsell or a request for anything. It was just a simple check-in with no agenda. It wasn't huge, but it felt positive – proactive, even – and that was new.

The following two days passed quietly. Sophie didn't try to force big changes, but something had definitely shifted. She stopped pretending she didn't have time to think. She noticed the way she defaulted to checking her inbox instead of planning. She even caught herself about to say yes to a quick-turnaround, low-price job that would not only throw off her week, but likely frustrate and demoralise her in the process, and said no.

Small things.

Each time she opened the notebook, she felt the discomfort prodding at her. But instead of ignoring it, she gave it ten minutes. Just ten. Enough to acknowledge what was in her head. She didn't try to solve everything at once; she just kept noticing and naming what she was avoiding. Each time, the bigger picture got clearer.

One afternoon, she wrote:

> I've built something that needs me constantly.
>
> I'm scared of stepping back in case it stops working.
>
> I've been measuring progress by busyness, not direction or steps towards a goal.
>
> Do I even have a clear goal?!

She closed the notebook and reflected. No answers yet, but more clarity than she'd had in months, and that felt like progress.

• • •

Katie's face appeared on the screen just after 10am. Her relaxed smile suggested she was in no rush. She'd suggested a catch-up call to keep Sophie accountable and moving forward. 'A mug of tea in hand as usual, I see,' she said, grinning.

Sophie lifted her mug. 'Never without.'

Katie leaned forwards slightly. 'OK, Soph, you've done the hard bit. Most people never stop long enough to get honest about what they're avoiding. But now you've named the storm, the next thing is to get a little perspective on it.'

She picked up her book and turned to a page marked with a sticky tab. 'Fear has this habit of making things feel bigger than they are. So we shrink. We stall. We go quiet and don't even try. And then, the thought of these things can become worse than doing them.'

She held up her copy of *Be More Buffalo,* the cover creased, spine softened. 'This book changed things for me because it taught me tools I could actually use. Not theory. Not fluff. Just…perspective and action.'

She flipped it open. 'One of the most useful pages? This one: "Best/Worst/Most Likely tool". It's a simple exercise that nudges your brain past the panic.'

She typed it into the chat box.

Best Case

Worst Case

Most Likely Case

'You take a fear or a decision you're avoiding and write all three. It forces your brain to look past the panic and see the situation clearly.'

Sophie nodded. 'OK…so for raising my prices?'

Katie smiled. 'Perfect one. Let's try it now. You go first.'

Sophie opened a fresh page in her notebook.

> Fear: Raising my rates.
>
> Best Case: They agree straight away. Respect the new rate. Recommend me to others.
>
> Worst Case: They leave. Complain. I lose the income.
>
> Most Likely: One or two ask questions. A couple say no. Some say yes. I feel nervous but realise it was worth it.

She read them aloud.

Katie nodded. 'Exactly. Now it's no longer a vague fear; it's a decision with range. And from there, you can make a move.'

Sophie looked down at her notes. 'This actually helps,' she said, feeling a tingle of hope in her gut. 'It gives the fear edges. Makes it less…scary!'

Katie closed her book. 'Do one of these a day. Doesn't need to be big. One fear. One page. Just keep going. Fear gets quieter when you start moving… taking action.'

• • •

Later that day, Sophie sat at her desk with the notebook open. The cursor blinked on what should have been a social post but was currently a taunting blank screen. She had written and deleted the opening line three times already.

Katie's voice echoed. *Fear gets quieter when you start moving.*

After scribbling this reminder on a Post-it note and slapping it onto the wall above her laptop, Sophie flipped through her notebook to reread what she'd written earlier.

> Fear: Posting something about my real work, not just finished designs.
>
> Best Case: It resonates. Someone gets in touch. I feel proud.
>
> Worst Case: It falls flat. I feel exposed. I overthink it all evening.
>
> Most Likely: A few people notice. Maybe one comment. But I feel better for doing it.

She clicked back to the post. This time, she kept it simple.

> Most of my work starts long before the design. Strategy. Clarity. Brand thinking. I used to lead this with a team. Now I do it solo. But I'm moving towards something that is better structured and more collaborative. If you're building something that needs stronger brand thinking, let's talk.

She didn't overedit or polish the language. She just posted it. Then she stood up, made a cup of tea and took herself off for a screen break.

When she returned ten minutes later, a message was waiting for her. It was from an old client, asking if she had time for a call next week.

Sophie's stomach did a little flip. Not because the message was life-changing, but because it felt like proof that she was moving and something was moving back.

That evening, Sophie opened up the notebook again. At the top of the page, she wrote:

> What I did today that scared me:
>
> – Posted something honest
>
> – Showed up as a strategist, not just a designer
>
> – Didn't wait until it was perfect
>
> What happened:

– One message

– No drama

– A small win

She closed the notebook, felt a slight stirring of, what was it…pride? Positivity? Whatever it was, she liked it and wanted more. Not every fear needs a big response. Sometimes it just needs proof that the world won't end when you stop hiding.

•••

It was late. The house was quiet. The kids were in their rooms, headphones on, chatting with friends or gaming, bedroom doors closing everyone else out.

Sophie sat on the sofa, scrolling without really taking anything in.

Then she stopped.

One of her old contacts, Emma, had just posted about launching a new creative studio. They'd worked together years ago on a large rebrand project when Sophie was still leading a team at the agency. Emma had gone freelance a year later and always seemed a step or two ahead.

Sophie stared at the post for a moment, then tapped through to the profile. She hovered over the message button.

It felt awkward. She hadn't spoken to Emma in over a year, but she knew what she needed. Not a pitch or a favour. Just a conversation with someone who got it. She opened the message window and typed:

> Hey Emma, I saw your recent post. Your studio looks brilliant. Would you be up for a catch-up sometime soon? I'm reshaping a few things in my business and could really use a fresh perspective. Coffee's on me if you're local, or happy to Zoom if that's easier.

She read it once, then hit send. It was time to start paying it forward.

That was it.

The fear hadn't disappeared. She just didn't let it stop her this time.

Action steps: Overcome fear and procrastination

This chapter is about turning awareness into movement. Not big leaps, just intentional small steps in the right direction. Use the prompts below to move through fear instead of waiting for it to disappear.

1. Name the fear clearly

Choose one thing you've been avoiding in your business. Write it at the top of the page. Keep it simple and specific.

Examples could include: 'Raising my rates', 'Launching a new offer', 'Saying no to a draining client'.

2. Use the Best/Worst/Most Likely tool

Draw three columns as below and answer the questions about the thing you wrote at the top of the page.

Best Case	**Worst Case**	**Most Likely**
What's the ideal outcome?	What's the realistic worst-case scenario?	What is most probable?

You'll often realise the worst isn't as bad as it felt.

3. Create a fear/action list

Draw two columns and give them the following headings:

- What I'm Afraid Of
- What I Can Do Anyway

Then, jot down your answers. Examples could include:

- If I promote myself, I'll come across as too confident.
- Post something useful or honest.

4. Take one step

Pick one action from your list of things you can do anyway, and do it today. The list might include:

- Send the message.
- Say no.
- Ask.
- Begin.

Then write down what happened – not just the result, but how it felt.

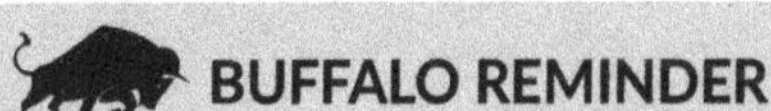

Fear will show up. That means you're moving out of your comfort zone.

Don't wait until you feel ready.

Start small.

Even the smallest action cuts through anxiety more than overthinking ever will.

To access extra resources, scan the QR code below, or go to www.bemorebuffalo.com.

THREE

The First Downpour

The message came in just after lunch.

> Appreciate the call, Sophie, but we've decided to go with a bigger agency for now. Hope we can work together another time.

Sophie read it twice, then closed her inbox. It was a polite brush-off, but better than being ghosted, she supposed. Still, the heaviness of rejection lodged itself like a rock in her stomach.

The project itself hadn't really excited her. Sure, the money would be nice, but deep down, Sophie knew that after the small wins of the past few days, she'd been looking forward to feeling that momentum grow.

She sat back in her chair with a heavy sigh. *Maybe this is why I don't reach out more,* she thought, *why I stay hidden in the safe zone, waiting for work to just come to me, instead of actively seeking it out. Less expectation means less chance of feeling like this.*

Feeling the need to vent, she opened her notebook. For a few minutes, she just stared at the blank page. Then she wrote one word at the top:

Setback

Underneath it, she listed:

Reached out

Showed up

Got a no

She wanted to stop there – close the book, bury her feelings and walk away from the discomfort – but something in her paused. Katie had said something during a group call last year that came back to her now: *Your ability to move forward depends less on how often you win, and more on how you respond when you don't.*

She flipped back to earlier pages, scanning the words. The storm. The fears. The first steps. *This is part of it,* she thought. *It's not failure, it's just feedback.*

Sophie snapped the notebook shut with new resolve to view this no as feedback and get on with her day. Yet that heavy rock still niggled, tugging at her energy and focus.

•••

That evening, a voice note arrived from Katie.

> *Hey, you might hit a dip this week. It's normal, but it's the bit nobody talks about. I want to give you a tool I still use every time something doesn't turn out the way I hoped. It's simple. Four steps: Pause, Observe, Decide, Act. I call it the PODA reset.*

Katie continued:

> *When something knocks you back, don't spiral, just pause. Observe what actually happened. Fact, not feeling. Then decide what your next step is, and act. Doesn't matter how small. The most resilient people I know aren't emotionally bulletproof. They just don't get stuck for long. They keep moving.*

Katie seemed to have a sixth sense. How did she always know exactly what Sophie needed at the exact right time?

Sophie grabbed her notebook and wrote down the steps.

P – Pause

Notice what just happened. Let yourself feel it, no rush to fix.

O – Observe

What truly happened? What did you control? What did you learn?

D – Decide

What now? What matters next?

A – Act

Take a small, clean action. Move something forward.

She opened her laptop and looked at the rejection email again. OK, so they had said no. It was just business, and she could spend some time considering why they felt a bigger agency was a better fit, maybe even ask them for feedback. She drummed her fingers on the laptop and thought about what small action she could take now to keep moving forward.

Then she clicked to compose a new email and sent a short note to check in with an old client she'd got on well with. She'd been meaning to reconnect for months but hadn't got round to it. It wasn't a pitch, nor were her words weighted with desperation. The email was short and friendly. A genuine 'How are things?'

She picked up a pen and added one more line to the previous notebook page about today's setback:

> I took action anyway. Not for results, just to keep going.

•••

Early the next morning, Sophie checked her emails before she was fully awake. One stood out: a reply from someone she'd pitched to a few weeks ago. She'd followed up twice and heard nothing. Now this:

> Thanks, Sophie, but we've gone in another direction.

That made two noes in less than forty-eight hours.

She sat at the kitchen table, tea cooling beside her. Frustration started to build. Why bother?

A text message popped up. Katie again.

> Read this today and thought of you. Ever read Go For No!? The whole idea is to shift how you view rejection. Most people stop after one or two noes and think they're failing. But the most successful people know that the noes are all part of it. They even go looking for them! Every no means you're taking action. You're in motion.

Sophie tapped the link to an online bookseller and skimmed the summary of *Go For No!*. A line jumped out: 'Yes is the destination. No is how you get there.'

She reread it, then picked up her notebook.

Go for No

2 noes

No disasters

Still here

She thought about how hard she'd been taking rejection. How personal it felt. How quickly it would knock her off course and cause her to retreat into herself, scared to feel that way again.

She decided to change that as of now. The sting was still there from the two rejections, but now she had a different perspective. She didn't need everyone to say yes; she needed to keep showing up until the right people did.

• • •

The rest of the week was quieter. No breakthroughs or big wins, but something significant in Sophie had changed.

Each morning, she opened her notebook and wrote a few lines to check in and keep herself accountable and focused on moving forward.

How did I move forward today?

What knocked me?

What did I learn?

What's next?

She found herself using the PODA reset most days, almost without thinking. One line in particular seemed to make the biggest difference: 'What did I control?' Often, the answer was something small and simple.

I showed up.

I sent the message.

I followed through.

Seeing a growing list of actions she'd taken in the face of disappointment was starting to rebuild her confidence.

By Friday afternoon, Sophie had read Katie's message about *Go For No* three times. That one line from the summary kept playing on repeat in her mind: 'Yes is the destination. No is how you get there.'

It made sense now.

She'd spent too long treating every no as a sign to stop. As if rejection meant she was wrong, too late or not good enough. Now she saw it differently. No wasn't the end, it was part of the road.

An idea popped into her head. She could turn this into a challenge – see how many noes she could get in the next month. She pulled her chair in, opened a fresh page and wrote across the top:

Go for No – 30 days

Then she drew three columns and gave them each a heading:

Follow Up With

Meet for Coffee

Collaborate With

Without overthinking it, she started listing names. Some were from old enquiries; some were people who had mentioned working together; others were contacts she respected but had never reached out to. Seventeen names were on the page by the time she finished.

She looked at the list, pleased. Instead of feeling pressured or worried, she saw the potential opportunities in front of her.

Underneath, she wrote:

> Rejection doesn't mean I'm doing it wrong.
>
> Avoiding action is costing more than a no ever could.
>
> I can build resilience by stacking actions.

She closed the notebook.

Sophie was done hiding and holding herself back. She wasn't about to start pestering and chasing these people, but she would be putting herself out there. One message, one meeting, one conversation at a time.

•••

It was late afternoon when the reply came in. Sophie had just come back from a walk and was scrolling through her inbox without expecting much.

> Subject: Re: Strategy Session Follow-Up

She opened it.

> Hey Sophie, thanks for checking in. I've been meaning to come back to you. Are you free next Wednesday? I'd love to talk about how we can move forward with the brand refresh.

She read it twice. Then a third time. It was from someone she'd given a quote to two months ago, but since then she'd heard nothing. She'd assumed it was a dead lead, but their name was on her Go for No challenge list, so she'd followed up anyway – not with any expectation or emotion attached, just as part of the process.

Now here it was. A yes! Or the beginning of one, anyway. Sophie smiled to herself and felt that flicker of hope spark to life in her stomach.

She replied with her availability, hit send and reached for her notebook. At the bottom of the 'Go for No' page, she wrote:

+ 1 yes

From a follow-up I nearly didn't send!

Then she headed to the kitchen to make a cup of tea and sit for a minute. No laptop or phone, just taking a quiet moment to reflect and notice what had changed. Not everything – not yet – but enough to feel the difference.

Her fear was still there, but smaller. Her doubts hadn't vanished, but they weren't leading the way. And for the first time in a long time, her direction didn't feel reactive. It felt chosen.

• • •

That evening, Sophie was scrolling through old project folders from past clients: visuals, guidelines and entire brand strategies, all created from scratch.

A folder labelled 'Studio Ideas' caught her eye and she opened it, knowing this particular project was a little closer to home. Inside were half-finished designs for her own brand: colour palettes, messaging samples and a draft slide deck for her positioning.

She clicked through the files. Each was a reminder of how she had used to feel about her work and her intention when she set up her business. It was never just about making things look good. It was about shaping how businesses show up, lead and grow.

She realised she'd got caught up in taking whatever jobs came along to pay the bills, and had lost sight of her vision. She'd been hiding behind client work. Not because she didn't believe in herself, but because showing up as herself made her feel exposed – vulnerable, even.

That was the next storm. Not pricing. Not proposals. Visibility.

She opened her notebook again.

> What storm am I facing next?
>
> Being seen. Not just as helpful or reliable, but truly seen for what I can do.

Knowing it was time to lead by example and walk her talk, she wrote at the top of a clean page:

Decision:

To stop waiting until it's perfect.

To use my own tools, not just teach them.

To treat my brand like it matters. Because it does.

She closed all her tabs – client work, admin, distractions – and opened a blank document. Brand identity. Offer. Strategy.

Not for a pitch. Not to meet a deadline. This time, the brief was her own, and for once, it wasn't at the bottom of the list.

It felt good to choose her own business. To make herself the priority. To show up.

Action steps: Build resilience

This chapter is about building resilience in the face of adversity and challenges. Use these tools to recover from setbacks with clarity instead of collapse.

1. Try the PODA reset

When something knocks you off track, write this in your notebook:

- **Pause** – What just happened? Let yourself feel it.
- **Observe** – What are the facts? What did you learn?
- **Decide** – What now? What matters most?
- **Act** – What's one small thing you can do to move forward?

2. Create your Go for No list

Draw three columns and give them the following headings:

- People to Follow Up With
- People to Meet for a Conversation
- People to Collaborate With

Jot down a few people below each heading. Reach out to them and track the responses you receive: the noes and the yeses. Let both move you forward.

3. Prioritise your own business

Treat your brand like a client project. Define your message. Shape your identity. Speak up. No more hiding behind the work.

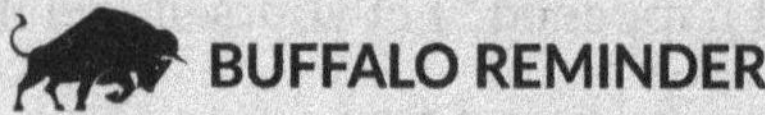

Resilience isn't about pushing through without feeling.

It's about moving again after the hit.

Keep showing up. Keep walking forward.

The storm is part of it – but so is your strength.

To access extra resources, scan the QR code below, or go to www.bemorebuffalo.com.

FOUR

The Eye of The Storm

Monday morning, 8.45am. The café was quieter than usual. There were a couple of freelancers with laptops, the clatter of cups behind the counter, but not much else. Sophie arrived early, but Katie was already there, at the same table, with the same calm presence. Two mugs sat between them. One was clearly for Sophie.

'I thought we'd start the week properly,' Katie said. 'No inbox. No calls. Just some space to think.'

Sophie put her bag down and wrapped her hands around the mug of hot tea. 'I did something this morning,' she said. 'Nothing major, but it feels positive.'

Katie raised an eyebrow.

Sophie pulled her notebook from her bag, found the page she wanted and slid it across the table.

What do I want to happen next?

Katie read the list while Sophie sipped her tea.

- 3 retained clients who value strategy
- 1 brand workshop per month
- A small, focused team by year end
- Speaking at two creative business events
- A brand and website that reflect where I'm heading

'Nice!' Katie said. 'It's clear and sounds like it's from the heart, not what someone told you to want.'

Sophie beamed and flipped the page for Katie to continue reading.

What could I do this week to move towards that?

- Reach out to a local business meetup organiser
- Draft an outline for a brand workshop
- Follow up with two people from the Go for No list

– Write a post about the benefits of brand strategy

– Block time to work on the studio brand

'I'm not trying to do it all at once,' she said. 'I'm just focused on keeping moving, one page at a time.'

Katie grinned, a flash of pride in her eyes. 'That's how it's done.'

There was a comfortable silence between the two before Sophie asked, 'Can I ask how you learned all this? The frameworks, the questions. Did someone teach you?'

Katie set her mug down. 'I was where you are, not so long ago.'

'Really?!' Sophie felt shocked; Katie seemed like she'd always had this calm, confident success.

'Yep. I was totally overwhelmed. On paper, I was doing well, but I felt like I was pushing everything uphill all by myself. I'd left a job that paid well to do something I cared about, and I didn't realise just how isolating that would feel.'

Sophie nodded. 'Mmm, I know that feeling.'

Katie continued: 'Then I met this guy, Dan. He invited me to a business meetup. I was a bit reluctant, to be honest. Thought it would just be a load of strangers all touting for business.'

She paused, reflecting on what she had almost missed out on.

'But I went, and it changed everything. It wasn't just another pitch fest. Everyone was so welcoming, and they were all asking questions and supporting each other. I loved how genuine it felt.'

Sophie leaned in. 'So, what exactly was it?'

'It was a proper community. The kind that helps you keep going when things wobble. Dan used to say something again and again until it stuck…'

She pulled a worn flyer from her notebook and handed it to Sophie. At the top, in bold font, it said: '**Friendship Fuels Business**'.

'I've kept this since that first meeting,' Katie said. 'Because it's true. It's why I make time for people like you.'

Sophie looked down at the flyer and felt a spark of realisation. She didn't have to go it alone. Katie hadn't, and maybe that's why she was always so calm and happy.

•••

Sophie was back at her desk by 2.12pm. The house was quiet. She glanced at the Post-it note above her laptop: 'Fear gets quieter when you start moving.' Now, tea brewed and notebook open, she started to write:

1. Do two quick follow-ups from the Go for No list

Done. Simple check-ins.

2. Reach out to the local business meetup organiser

She opened LinkedIn and messaged Natalie, who ran the group.

> Hi Natalie, I've heard good things about your online events. I'm a brand strategist looking to connect more locally and would love to learn more.

Then she wrote another idea in her notebook.

3. Write a piece of content

She opened a clean document and typed:

> Most people think brand design is just logos and colours. But without a strategy, it's just decoration. If you're in that messy middle space – growing, shifting or stuck – I'd love to hear from you. That's the space I work best in.

Saved. Maybe posted tomorrow. Three actions, no overthinking, no emotional attachment. Just done and keeping things moving forward.

Later that week, Sophie saw a post on Instagram from Jordan, a copywriter she hadn't spoken to in over a year. It looked slick, but something about it felt a little forced. She decided to reach out:

> Hey Jordan. Totally random, but how are you? Fancy a catch-up this week?

He replied within hours.

> Honestly, that means a lot. I'd love that. Free Thursday morning?

They met in the same café as where Sophie had met Katie.

'Appreciate you reaching out,' Jordan said. 'Most people just see your posts and assume everything's fine.'

Sophie nodded. 'I know, and is it…fine?'

Jordan looked down, 'To be totally honest, Soph, I've been short of work. I'm not panicking just yet, but if something doesn't come in soon, I may be. I've got a proposal to do for a sustainability brand. It's a really exciting project, but I feel a bit stuck with it. They want something innovative, maybe incorporating AI, something new. But I've no idea where to start.'

'Ah, that's a tough one.' Sophie could sympathise. Working solo meant you often felt you couldn't fulfil the brief properly.

'Want me to take a look?' she offered.

Jordan's eyes lit up at the offer as he pulled up the email on his phone.

Sophie read the brief. 'OK, you're right about them wanting something different,' she said. 'So…what if you don't pitch it alone?'

Jordan looked up, brows knitted together in confusion. 'What do you mean?'

'Well, you've got messaging, I've got creativity. Let's add someone who understands AI and emerging tech. Then pitch it as a team.'

'You know someone?'

She smiled, pulling out her phone to make a call. 'I know someone who might!'

Katie answered immediately.

Sophie explained the brief, the idea and the gap they wanted to fill.

Katie didn't pause. 'I know the perfect person! Her name's Leena, she works a lot with AI and purpose-led projects. I'll do an intro now.'

Then she added, 'But, Sophie, pitch it properly. Not three different proposals. Show up as a team.'

• • •

The next day, Sophie and Jordan met with Leena on Zoom to shape the proposal. They clicked quickly, each bringing a different strength to the table. Sophie mapped out the creative approach, Jordan worked on how to position it clearly and persuasively, and Leena brought fresh, practical ideas for how AI could enhance the client's customer experience.

By the end of the call, they had an outline for a sharp, considered proposal that felt exciting and different, but doable. And they'd built it as a team.

'You know,' Jordan said, 'this is the first pitch I've enjoyed in months.'

Sophie nodded. 'I feel the same. I'd forgotten how much I love being part of a team and not carrying everything alone.'

That night, curled on the sofa with her notebook open, Sophie reviewed the goals she'd written that Monday. Each one was ticked.

It felt good to see the progress, but what stayed with her wasn't the checklist. It was how she felt. She hadn't just moved things forward. She'd started to build something alongside people who brought out her best. She'd shown up, followed through and shared the load with others.

She hadn't reached the other side of the storm yet, but she wasn't standing still. And for the first time in a long time, she wasn't walking into it alone.

At the bottom of the page, she wrote:

> Be More Buffalo – Don't do it alone. Move with the herd.

Action steps: Create clear goals and small wins

This chapter is about replacing vague ambition with focused movement. Don't just hope progress will happen. Make it visible. Make it practical. Make it yours. Use the following steps to help you work towards this.

1. Use the CLEAR framework for goal setting

C – Clearly define the outcome

L – Link it to your purpose

E – Establish milestones

A – Create action steps for this week

R – Review and adjust weekly

2. Focus on small wins

Write one simple task per day that moves your bigger goal forward. Complete it before anything else.

3. Build your weekly momentum list

At the start of the week, write the answers to these questions:

- What do I want to happen next?
- What actions can I take this week to move towards taking them?

Review and tick off as you go.

4. Reach out to someone

Check in with someone in your network with no agenda – just a genuine 'How are you?'

5. Collaborate on a next step

Don't do it all alone. Pick one goal you've been stuck on and ask: 'Who could help me move this forward?'

BUFFALO REMINDER

Small wins are far from small. Each one is a sign of movement, direction and progress. Build them daily, and the big wins will follow.

To access extra resources, scan the QR code below, or go to www.bemorebuffalo.com.

FIVE

Run With The Herd

Monday morning again. The Post-it note had lost its stick and fallen off the wall, but its message had settled somewhere deeper. Sophie no longer needed a reminder to act. She was already doing it daily without overthinking.

A reply from Natalie was waiting for Sophie in her inbox. Natalie explained the format of her online networking sessions, and after a brief back-and-forth, Sophie was booked onto the next one and had also invited Jordan along.

She was already thinking about people and connections, and while she did this, she opened her notebook to a new page and wrote at the top:

Who do I already know?

This time, the focus wasn't on pitching. It was on the people themselves. People she had come across who she liked and respected, and would like to build or deepen a relationship with.

She gave herself ten minutes and wrote names without filtering: past clients, fellow freelancers, old colleagues and creatives she admired from afar. Even those people she'd met once and never followed up with.

When she stopped, there were twenty-three names. Next to each, she added a quick note:

- Message this week
- Invite for coffee
- Just check in
- Ask about their next launch

It was time to build a stronger network around her, starting with reconnecting with people she already knew.

• • •

Later that day, Sophie opened a voice note from Katie.

Hey, something I thought might help as you start reconnecting. It's a visual I go back to a lot. Think of your network in three layers, like circles around you. The closer the circle, the more consistent the relationship and, usually, the more meaningful the opportunities.

Sophie listened, pen hovering over her notebook at the ready.

The inner circle is your Five. These are the people you speak to regularly. They know what you're building, what you care about and they'd probably recommend you without thinking. You can send them a voice note and it won't be weird.

Then there's your Fifteen. These are people who trust you but maybe don't hear from you much. They respect your work, you've probably helped each other before, but you're not front of mind. This group has huge potential if you just reconnect with consistency.

And then your outer circle, your Fifty. These are more like acquaintances, friendly contacts, people you'd say hi to at an event. You're in their world, but only just.

You don't need hundreds of people. You need depth. The goal is to move the right people from the outer circles inwards gradually.

Sophie returned to the start and listened again. This time she sketched the circles into her notebook:

The Five. The Fifteen. The Fifty.

She looked at the list she'd written that morning, twenty-three names, and began to mark them up. A few were clear candidates for her Five. A handful were a solid Fifteen. Most sat on the edge.

Then she wrote at the bottom of the page:

> It's not about more. It's about closer.

It made perfect sense. Collecting acquaintances was pointless if you never invested in building trusting relationships with anyone.

• • •

Natalie's Zoom meeting ran like clockwork. There were eighteen people on the call – enough to feel lively, but not overwhelming.

It wasn't like the other online networking events Sophie had dipped into before. There were no egos, no endless pitching. People actually listened to each other, and the conversations felt natural, not forced. It was the kind of space where people got to know each other, rather than just talking at each other.

Jordan had joined, too. They'd messaged beforehand, and as the session began, they both settled in with open curiosity about the event.

Sophie scanned the names and faces on the call and discovered Leena was also there. She excitedly messaged Jordan:

> Leena's here!

He replied:

> Ha! Small world. She's everywhere at the moment. Love it.

Midway through, Natalie introduced a short guest segment. 'This week we've got Leena Nair with us,' she said. 'Leena helps small businesses apply AI in practical, thoughtful ways – especially when it comes to branding, content and client delivery.'

Leena spoke clearly and simply. There were no buzzwords or jargon, just helpful ideas. It was obvious she understood how to make complicated things feel workable.

After the session, Sophie sent her a message:

> Great to see you again! Your segment was brilliant. Let's catch up soon.

Leena replied five minutes later:

> Ahh, thank you! And yes, I'd love that!

Another message popped up on-screen: a new group chat with Sophie, Jordan and Leena and a message from Jordan.

> Hey! Just letting you know we have a date to pitch! It's in a couple of weeks.

Sophie's heart gave a little flutter of excitement. A small win and an opportunity to pitch something special as part of a team again. All because she'd opened her eyes to the bigger picture and the people around her.

• • •

The next day followed the usual pattern of bickering teenagers, last-minute school forms and a chaotic kitchen, but there was one difference. Sophie wasn't dragging herself through the morning. She hadn't woken with that tight, anxious feeling. It wasn't because her to-do list was empty, but because she no longer felt like she was carrying it all alone.

As she stirred milk into her tea, her son looked up from the table.

'You're smiley this week,' he said casually.

'Am I?'

'Yeah. Like, even when nothing's happening.'

'Yeah, I've noticed that too,' her daughter joined in with a cheeky grin. 'Something we should know about?'

'No, I just...feel good!' Sophie grinned and let the comment sink in. She'd been feeling the small changes, but having others notice was the confirmation she hadn't known she'd needed.

Thursday afternoon brought a sharp reminder that growth isn't always smooth. A retained client emailed to say they were pausing the contract.

> We love your work, but cash flow's a bit tight right now. Nothing personal.

It still felt like a kick in the gut.

For a few seconds, Sophie just sat there. She could feel that familiar tug of panic and self-doubt, the urge to catastrophise.

But this time, she caught it. She opened her notebook and used the PODA reset to jot down some thoughts.

> What has happened?
>
> What can I learn?
>
> What now?
>
> What small action can I take to move forward?

The act of writing slowed her brain, calmed her breathing and anchored her. Still, the wobble lingered, so she messaged Jordan.

Bit of a knock today. You free for a quick chat?

He called her two minutes later. She filled him in, trying to keep it light. He didn't rush to fix it; he just listened and asked good questions, letting the silence do some of the work.

'That sucks,' he said finally. 'But it's not a reflection of your work. It's a cash flow thing. You said it yourself.'

'I know,' she said. 'But knowing it and feeling it – still not quite the same.'

'True. But look, you're already handling it differently. That's a big shift.'

She let that sink in.

By the time they ended the call, the sting hadn't disappeared, but the story she was telling herself about it had. She wasn't spiralling. She wasn't alone. And she still had momentum.

Later that evening, she messaged Katie.

Lost a client today. But weirdly, it didn't undo me.

Katie replied:

> Was it PLU?

Sophie stared at the message and asked:

> PLU?

Sophie explained.

> People Like Us. People you love working with, could go for a drink with and chat easily to. They just get you and value what you bring. People you'd want three more of.

Sophie thought for a moment. Then she typed back:

> No. They weren't. They were draining, always asking for more and ignoring boundaries. I think this is actually good news.

Katie replied once more:

> There it is. As you get more clarity and direction in your business, the wrong people will naturally drift away and make space for those who are PLU.

• • •

Friday morning. The house was quiet after the chaos of getting the kids out the door. Sophie sat at her desk with a hot cup of tea, scrolling through her LinkedIn feed. Not mindlessly, but with intent. She wasn't there to post; she was there to engage with others' posts.

'I know a lot of people,' she thought out loud. Only, she didn't really *know* them; they were just acquaintances – but that could start to change with instigating some intentional interactions instead of just posting.

She started small. A thoughtful comment on a post by another brand strategist, someone she'd heard speak at an online summit but never properly engaged with. Then another comment. Then a message to someone she hadn't spoken to in over a year: a copywriter she had used to chat to in a group she'd quietly left.

> Hey, saw your update on client onboarding, really loved your point about setting boundaries upfront. Let me know if you ever fancy a virtual coffee sometime.

They were seemingly small acts, but each one built towards a deeper connection and started to move people from her outer circle closer to her.

Later that afternoon, Sophie remembered Natalie's meeting. She'd met quite a few great people, but now she wondered if there was something she could do to help one or two of them.

She found her notes and was reminded that two people in particular had stood out: Zara, a marketing strategist working with ethical fashion brands, and Max, a product designer pivoting into UX. Both had mentioned needing support or new connections. She scanned her contacts to see if she could connect them with anyone and found Olivia, a creative producer working with fashion clients, and Tom, UX lead at a digital agency hiring freelancers.

Perfect! She sent two short messages:

> Hey Zara, not sure if this is useful, but I know a creative producer working with the same clients as you. Would you like an intro?

> Hey Max, I remember what you said in the session –there's someone in my network who's looking for UX support. Want me to connect you?

She smiled. It had only taken a few minutes, but it felt surprisingly good to show up for other people.

She had used to do this all the time. She wasn't sure when or why she'd stopped. Maybe it was the weight of running her own business, or just the speed of everything. It was easy to get swept along in the busyness and forget to look up.

Now that she had, she remembered how powerful it was. A small, simple action. She hadn't realised how much she'd missed it and how much things like this mattered.

• • •

On Monday afternoon, a message popped up from Zara:

> Thanks again for the intro to Olivia. We had a great call this morning, and she mentioned someone else who might need brand support. I passed your name on, hope that's OK?

Sophie blinked. She hadn't expected anything in return, and the kindness caught her off guard in the best way.

A few minutes later, Max messaged:

> Appreciate the intro to Tom. Looks like something's happening there. Also, your website's great! Did you write your own copy?

She was surprised: not at the compliment, but at how different things felt when she led with generosity, not desperation.

She opened her journal and wrote:

> This is how it works. Not always fast or obvious, but steady.
>
> Give. Connect. Show up. Repeat.

And below that:

Be More Buffalo. Relationships create more opportunities and move things forward.

Tuesday morning arrived, and Sophie was ready for the day: tea in hand, notebook open. She turned back to the diagram she'd sketched from Katie's voice note last week:

The Five. The Fifteen. The Fifty, a rhythm for relationships.

At the time, it had felt interesting. Now it felt important. She could see it more clearly.

Her Five weren't all current.

Her Fifteen had potential.

Her Fifty held more opportunity than she'd ever noticed.

What she needed was a regular plan to connect with these people and keep moving them closer. She flipped to a clean page and wrote:

The F network

- *Every week: Check in with at least two of the Five.*

- *Every two weeks: Reconnect with two of the Fifteen.*

- Every month: Message or comment meaningfully with ten of your Fifty.
- Bonus: Make one introduction or share something useful.

This wasn't about sticking to a rigid system or cramming more tasks into her week. It was about creating an intentional habit that would continue to strengthen the relationships within her network.

Action steps: Build relationships that grow your business

You already know more people than you think. The goal isn't to collect contacts, it's to connect with intention and then deepen those relationships. This chapter is about seeing your network more clearly, and tending to it with purpose, not pressure. Below are some ideas to help you do this.

1. Map your F Network™

Draw three concentric circles on a blank page. Label them:

- **The Five** – People who know what you're building and speak to you regularly
- **The Fifteen** – People who respect your work but don't hear from you often

- **The Fifty** – Friendly connections and acquaintances

Now list real names in each circle. Start with who comes to mind, and aim for at least three in each category. Don't force it, this is a working list, not a test.

2. Start a weekly relationship rhythm

Set a gentle, repeatable cadence for yourself. For example:

- **Each week**: Check in with two people from your Five.
- **Each fortnight**: Reconnect with one person from your Fifteen.
- **Each month**: Reach out meaningfully to someone in your Fifty.
- **Bonus**: Make one helpful introduction or share something valuable.

You can block time out in your calendar for this or set reminders, but remember: this isn't about doing it on autopilot or as a copy-and-paste task. It needs to be genuine and considered, something you *feel*, not just something you *do*.

3. Pay it forward this week

Look back through recent notes from conversations, events or posts. Who mentioned a challenge or goal? Offer something small but thoughtful: a useful article, a kind check-in or an introduction that might help.

Reach out to one person this week without expecting anything back. For example:

> Hey, I was thinking of you, I know someone who might be able to help. Would you like an intro?

These small gestures often mean more than you realise.

4. Ask yourself the PLU question

Review your current clients, collaborators and the people you spend time with. For each one, ask yourself: 'Is this person PLU?' People Like Us are those who value your work, get your style and energise rather than drain you.

If they aren't, that's OK. Not everyone will be the right fit. You don't need to chase people who drain you or try to convince the wrong ones to stay. Sometimes gaining clarity means letting some things go so you can make space for better things to come through, even when it comes to people.

BUFFALO REMINDER

Real relationships are built over time, not through transactions.

Storms are easier to face when you have people alongside you.

Keep showing up and making time and space for meaningful connection to take root.

Your network isn't just who you know, it's who you're building with.

To access extra resources, scan the QR code below, or go to www.bemorebuffalo.com.

SIX

A Break In The Clouds

The sun was already warming the kitchen tiles when Sophie sat down with her tea and opened her notebook. Things had felt steadier lately, calmer and more spacious. Not because everything was perfect, but because she no longer felt so isolated or stuck in her own head.

She'd been showing up more, listening, connecting, giving, and bit by bit, they were coming back – her voice, her confidence and her drive. She smiled to herself and marvelled at the profound impact a few simple tasks and using a notebook were having on her and her business.

Now it was time to go deeper. Not just to *do* the work, but to *own* what she stood for. She turned to a clean page and wrote at the top:

> What do I want to be known for?

Not what she could do.

Not what was listed on her services page.

Not even what paid the bills.

Katie's words from a recent catch-up call echoed in her mind:

> *You're not meant to be invisible. The people building real momentum in business, the ones who attract opportunities rather than chase them, decided to become known. To lead with who they are, not just what they do. That's influence.*

She'd nodded when Katie said it. They had been talking about becoming a Key Person of Influence, and it made perfect sense. Now, that idea niggled at her, urging her to define her message.

She thought about the projects she'd loved most – the ones where fast-growing businesses had lost clarity, outgrown their brand and needed help making sense of it all. That was her zone. Not just design, but realignment. Helping people reconnect with what matters and bring it to the surface.

She picked up her pen and wrote, slowly:

> I help values-led businesses in transition to define their purpose so they can lead, grow and communicate with clarity.

Three words stood out: Define. Lead. Communicate.

Sophie reread the words a few times; they felt like a good starting point. Writing them down gave her a clearer sense of direction, a simple anchor she could use when shaping her offer or making choices about how to show up.

Now Sophie had more clarity on what she really did, and for whom, the idea Katie had planted resurfaced: becoming a Key Person of Influence.

She'd dismissed it at first. Her mind had jumped to Instagram reels, viral TikToks and the kind of constant posting she had no interest in. She didn't want to be everywhere, sharing her entire life online and chasing likes, but now she understood it differently. Influence wasn't about visibility for the sake of it. It was about being clear, consistent and intentional. It was being the person others thought of *when it mattered*, when a specific need arose. If she was honest, she was still too hidden.

She flipped to a clean page in her notebook and wrote:

If I want to be seen as a Key Person of Influence, what needs to change?

- Speak more
- Share my thinking, not just finished work
- Say no to misaligned projects
- Be consistent
- Get in rooms where people value strategy, not just delivery

Then she added one more line, underlined:

Be known, not just seen

Natalie's group came to mind. That one Zoom session had already sparked two meaningful connections, and neither had felt forced. Maybe her influence didn't need to start with a stage. Maybe it could start there.

She messaged Natalie:

> Thanks again for the session. I've been thinking more seriously about speaking. Do you ever need contributors or guest speakers? Would love to help if the right fit comes up.

She hit 'Send' before she had a chance to overthink it. Then she sat back and smiled as she drank her tea, satisfied at yet another small step forward.

• • •

Natalie replied the next morning.

> Hey Sophie, I'd love that. I've got a seven-minute spotlight free at this week's session if you fancy it? We've got twelve people booked on.

Sophie smiled. It felt like perfect timing, almost as if the slot was waiting for her. Twelve people – a nice amount for her first talk. She messaged back:

> Count me in.

Sophie joined early to get settled and in the right state to present. Breakouts came first, and, again, the conversations flowed easily and the people were warm and relaxed.

In the first breakout session, someone shared that they were struggling to explain what they did now that their business had grown and evolved. Sophie made a mental note.

Then it was time for her talk. Seven minutes. No slides. Just her, a camera and her words.

'Thanks, Natalie. Hi everyone, I'm Sophie. I run a brand and design studio for values-led businesses who feel like their identity hasn't caught up with their growth.'

She paused and took a steadying breath so she didn't rush through the next bit.

'The people I love to work with are ambitious but grounded. They've built something real, often fast. But now they feel stuck. Their messaging is fuzzy. Their visuals no longer represent their work. They're respected, but not clearly understood.

'They often come to me saying things like "I've outgrown my brand" or "I can't explain what I do anymore." They're not after surface-level changes. They want to feel proud of how they show up and attract the right clients so they can step into their next stage of growth with credibility and ease.

'One of my recent clients had doubled her business in two years. But she was still using a brand she'd made on Canva in her kitchen. After six weeks of strategy and design, she raised her rates, landed her biggest client yet and told me she finally felt proud to share her website.

'So if you know someone who's outgrown how they show up, and wants their brand to reflect where they're going, I'd love to speak with them. Thanks for listening.'

There was a brief moment of silence before two people spoke, one after the other: 'That was incredibly clear. I've got someone I need to connect you with.'

'Same. I literally had this conversation with a client last week. You just described them.'

Sophie smiled and thanked them, doing her best to stay composed despite the quiet fizz of excitement rising in her chest. She hadn't expected it to land quite so well. Now she couldn't wait to do it again.

After the session, Sophie stayed on to thank Natalie directly.

'That was one of the clearest spotlights we've had in a long time,' Natalie said. 'You painted a real picture.'

Sophie smiled. 'Thanks for the opportunity. Honestly, it felt good to say it out loud finally. I've been working on making my message clearer, and I feel like it truly fits now.'

Natalie nodded, warm but thoughtful. 'Well, you sounded great, really confident and capable.'

Sophie paused, then added: 'If there's ever something I can do to support you or the group, let me know. I'd love to help in return.'

Natalie tilted her head as a flash of surprise lit up her face.

'You know, most people don't say that. They just take the slot and move on.'

Sophie shrugged gently. 'I've had a lot of help recently. Feels right to pass some of it on.'

Natalie smiled. 'I can see that. I'm always looking to meet more PLU.'

Sophie grinned in delight. 'People Like Us?'

'Exactly. Not lots of people, just the right ones. The ones who make the group stronger just by showing up.'

Sophie nodded. 'That's the kind of network I want to build and be part of, too. Let me know how I can join your group. I'd love to come regularly and get to know everyone.'

Sophie left the call excited to become a member, already planning on inviting a couple of people she'd reconnected with recently, too, who were PLU.

• • •

That night, Sophie reopened her notebook to read through her offer again. It still needed refining, but today had shown she was definitely on the right track. Her message had not only felt good to share publicly, but it had also landed well with the people in the room.

She scribbled a note at the bottom of the page:

> Today's version worked. I'm getting closer. Still not done.

Then:

> Ask for feedback: Katie, Jordan, Olivia.

She wasn't chasing compliments; she wanted honest feedback and a fresh perspective from people in her industry. The goal wasn't perfection; here, it was precision. A message sharp enough that the right people knew it was meant for them.

She tapped her pen once and added a final line:

> Keep testing. Keep listening. Keep showing up.

Refining her message wasn't a one-time task. It was something she would revisit, test and tweak consistently over the next few weeks to make sure what she landed on was right.

The next morning, Sophie opened her inbox and saw two new messages. Both were from people she'd met at Natalie's event. Each had the same tone: a genuine desire to help, with no expectation.

> Hi Sophie, I spoke to the person I mentioned yesterday. They were really interested in what you do. I explained the kind of businesses you work with, and they immediately said, 'That's what I need.' I'd like to make the intro properly. What's the best way for me to do that? Do you have a link to book a call or something you'd like me to send them?

Sophie read it twice. Then she clicked open the second message – almost identical.

> She asked if she could speak to you next week. Can I book something directly for you? Or do you want me to send them your calendar link?

Wow, this felt so easy. There was no chasing or awkward pitches. Just warm introductions and new doors being opened for her.

Sophie smiled as she copied her booking link, then she paused for a moment, before writing a short message she could save and reuse:

> Thanks for offering to make the intro. Here's my link to book a short call. Just let them know it's a twenty-minute session to see if it's a good fit. Relaxed, informative and absolutely no pressure.

She saved it, then copied the message and link into both replies. This was what it looked like when people really got what you did – not because you shouted louder, but because you made it easy to remember, repeat and refer.

For the first time in a long time, Sophie didn't feel like she was waiting to be discovered. She was being referred.

Action steps: Create a clear offer and invite opportunities

Being brilliant at what you do isn't enough. People need to understand it, and know how to talk about it when you're not in the room. This chapter is about getting clear on your offer, making it memorable and setting yourself up to receive referrals and invitations, and have conversations that count. Use these steps to help you.

1. Write the first clear version of your offer

On a blank page, answer these prompts as simply as possible:

- Who do you help? (Be specific. Name their stage, mindset or situation.)
- What do you help them with? (Focus on outcomes, not just deliverables.)
- Why does it matter? (What changes for them?)

Now shape it into one sentence that starts: 'I help…'. Remember, it doesn't need to be perfect on the first try, just honest and clear enough to test out.

2. Say it out loud

Share your new offer in one live conversation this week. It could be at a networking meeting, a coffee catch-up or even during a quick Zoom with a close business friend.

Pay attention to how it feels when you say it, and how people respond. Clarity gets noticed and remembered.

3. Make a 'referral-ready' follow-up message

Write a short message someone could use to introduce you. Include:

- Who you work with
- The kind of challenge you help solve
- A friendly link to a short call or contact page

An example might be:

> Sophie helps growing businesses that feel like they've outgrown their brand. She helps them define who they are and show up clearly as they grow. If that sounds useful, let me know and I can send you a link to book a call with her.

Save this. It will make it easier for people to refer you.

4. Ask for feedback from two to three trusted people

Pick people who will be honest. Send them your draft offer and ask:

- Does this sound like me?
- Is it clear who I work with and what I do?
- Can you think of someone who might need this?

Use the bits that land; don't do a complete U-turn, just make minor tweaks and refine gradually.

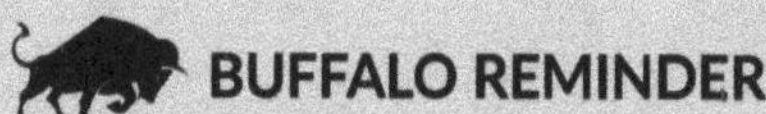

People can't send you opportunities if they don't understand what you do.

Say it clearly. Say it often. Say it in places where the right people are listening.

To access extra resources, scan the QR code below, or go to www.bemorebuffalo.com.

SEVEN

The Herd Holds Steady

Sophie's calendar was busier than it had been in months. Client calls, proposal chats, coffee catch-ups and two discovery sessions booked off the back of Natalie's event. All good things.

By Wednesday, though, she could feel it: the strain creeping in. The endless back-and-forth just to book a time. The Post-it notes multiplying across her desk. The proposal she'd promised to send on Monday that was still untouched, and three client projects underway but with no clear system holding it all together.

Her momentum wasn't gone, but it was starting to wobble.

Sophie headed to the kitchen to make her fourth cup of tea – and it was only 11am. As overwhelm threatened and fatigue stung her eyes, she remembered something Katie had said in a voice note the week before:

> *When things start working, most people stop showing up consistently. They get busy and go quiet, which causes the feast and famine we see and hear so much about. So this is the moment to do the opposite, and prepare for growth, not pull back. That's when you start building your team.*

Sophie had nodded at the time but brushed it off. It had felt too soon for that. Now it felt urgent.

This wasn't just a busy week; it was the beginning of something she'd been working towards. All of her actions over the last few weeks were to build something: a real business, a steady pipeline. If she waited for overwhelm to settle in before she looked for support, it would already be too late.

Building a team didn't have to mean employing people straight away; she could start with outsourcing to some trusted freelancers.

She opened her notebook and wrote:

> Who do I need in my virtual team?

I need to start having these conversations now, she thought, *not when it's too late to think.* She tapped her pen against the page. Instead of starting with job titles, she asked herself: 'Who do I already know that I'd want to work with again, or learn more about?'

Natalie's group had been full of people like that: kind, capable, with genuine energy. A different kind of room. A few names immediately sprang to mind: Leena – the AI specialist Katie had introduced. Someone who could strengthen her client work and proposals with ideas she'd never bring on her own. Rani – a virtual assistant she'd met briefly. Calm, organised, steady. Tom – a systems consultant she'd chatted to once. Someone who could help build simple automation for onboarding, file organisation and proposal follow-ups.

She flipped to a clean page and wrote:

> Potential Team – People I Already Know
>
> Leena – AI insights and innovation
>
> Rani – Scheduling, inbox, client support
>
> Tom – operations, backend systems, tools, automation

She wasn't about to outsource everything overnight. This was about starting small, building relationships now, so when the work did ramp up, she wouldn't be scrambling.

Underneath the list, she wrote:

Don't wait until you're drowning. Build the raft now.

She let that sink in, because she'd done that before, waited too long. Pushed through the overwhelm, convinced she could handle it all. But support isn't something you put in place *after* the storm hits; it's what keeps you steady *through* it.

She asked herself: 'Who would make the biggest difference right now?' The answer was clear, so that afternoon, she messaged Rani.

> Hi Rani, I've been thinking more about getting some help in place. Would love a quick chat to see how you work. No rush, just want to start the conversation.

It was one simple message, but it felt good to take steps towards growing a team and relieving some pressure on herself.

• • •

Later that week, Sophie opened a voice note from Katie.

> *Just checking in. I saw your post about creating space in your calendar. Looks like things are really moving. How's it going behind the scenes?*

Sophie replied with a quick update. Things were still shifting; she was gathering momentum and thinking ahead. She had even taken steps to build her support network, so she was feeling more organised than she had in months.

Katie replied, the genuine delight obvious in her voice.

> *That's amazing. You're looking at the bigger picture and building now, not just reacting day to day.*

Then she added:

> *I saw Dan at a meeting this week. You remember me telling you about him?*

Of course she did. Dan was the person who had invited Katie into a network years ago when she was overwhelmed and out on her own. He'd built a business community where people supported each other, built together and kept showing up through the mess.

Katie continued:

> *He reminded us that growing a sustainable business goes beyond growing a team. The people you have around you most often are important, and offer a totally different kind of support.*

Sophie nodded slowly. She'd been thinking the same thing. She pinged a message back to Katie:

> *Maybe it's time I looked into Dan's community properly. I think I'd like to be part of something like that.*

Another voice note arrived from Katie.

> *What is it you think you're missing?*

Sophie hesitated, then replied:

> *I guess… a place where people support each other, where I don't have to do all the thinking alone. Somewhere to be myself without always having to pitch.*

Katie replied:

> *And who have you had that with lately?*

Sophie thought for a moment, then answered:

> *Natalie. Jordan. You. Rani. Even Tom.*

Her voice slowed.

> *I'm already in it, aren't I?*

Katie's reply came with the sense of a smile in her tone.

> *You didn't need to find the right room. You just needed to realise you're already in it.*

Sophie sat back. All this time, she'd been trying to work out how to join something more collaborative – a place she could brainstorm and where she could show up exactly as she was – and it had been around her from the start.

She sat quietly after the voice note exchange, looking at the names in her notebook: the people she'd met, helped and reached out to. She thought about what people usually said: 'If you need clients, go networking.' It always made it sound so transactional, like the goal was to enter a room, find the buyer and close the deal. That wasn't what she'd found at all.

Yes, some might become clients, but the real value? That came from the ones who introduced her to others. Who offered perspective, challenged her thinking and made her braver. The ones who helped her show up on the days when she might have stayed quiet. That kind of room changed everything.

She saw her network no longer as a pipeline to manage, but as a community to nurture. It wasn't about hunting for clients or filling her calendar. What mattered now was surrounding herself with people who made the work better and the journey lighter.

She closed her notebook and smiled as final thoughts settled: *I'm not trying to outrun the storm anymore. I'm definitely being more buffalo. But more than that? I'm not doing it alone. I'm charging in with people beside me. And for the first time, it actually feels fun.*

Action steps: Strengthen your systems to scale what works

Momentum without structure creates stress. This chapter is your invitation to slow down – not to stop, but to stabilise. Strong systems and the right support help you scale without losing yourself in the process. Take the following five steps to help you achieve this.

1. Spot the strain

Write down three signs that you're hitting your limit. It might be:

- Forgetting follow-ups
- Losing track of proposals or projects
- Feeling like you can't respond properly to new opportunities

Name them. Then underline the one you've felt most this week. Awareness is the first step.

2. List your support gaps

Look at your week honestly. What are you still doing yourself that someone else could help with?

Common areas to consider are:

- Scheduling
- Proposal creation or formatting
- Inbox sorting or client comms
- Social media admin
- Follow-up or onboarding steps
- Content repurposing

Pick one area and commit to starting a conversation about it. You don't have to hire, just explore.

3. Map your virtual team

On a Page or Doc, create three columns with the following headings:

- What I Need Help With
- People I Know Who Could Help
- Next Step (Message, Research or Referral)

Think of people you've met at events, in groups or through mutual contacts and jot them down. Start with those you trust or want to learn more about.

4. Book one call this week

Reach out to someone you're considering for part of your virtual team. Use a no-pressure message. For example:

> Hey, I'm starting to look ahead and think about getting support in place as things grow. Would love a quick chat to understand what you offer and how it works.

You're not committing to anything, but it's the start of turning a job into a business.

5. Recognise the room you're already in

Take five minutes to reflect on the following questions:

- Who are the people supporting you already, through advice, introductions, encouragement or collaboration?
- What groups or events have felt energising, not draining?
- Where do you feel like you can be yourself?

Write your answers down.

You might not need to join something new; you might just need to show up more intentionally where you already are.

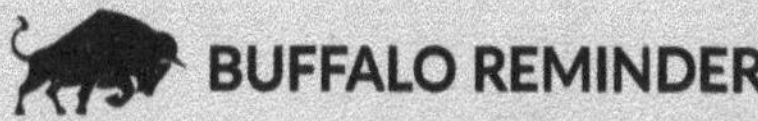

BUFFALO REMINDER

Don't wait until you're overwhelmed to build structure.

Strong systems are the foundation, not the reward.

Support doesn't slow you down, it lets you go further. Together.

To access extra resources, scan the QR code below, or go to www.bemorebuffalo.com.

EIGHT
Charging Through

It was still dark outside when Sophie opened her inbox. An email from one of her long-term PLU clients sat at the top, and the subject line was a pleasant surprise on a dark morning.

> Just wanted to share some good news...

She opened it with anticipation.

> Hey Sophie,
>
> So...the brand refresh is already landing better than I expected. We've had three new enquiries in a week, all from ideal clients!! Honestly, I've never felt this clear or confident pitching what we do.

> Thank you again. Working with you has changed everything.

Sophie sat back in her chair. It wasn't that she needed validation to know she was good at her work, but it was always great to hear feedback on the impact it had on her clients' businesses. The work she did went beyond visuals to give clear direction and confidence. More than that, it triggered the ripple effect that happens when people finally understand and articulate what they do properly, so that others do, too.

Sophie felt the win lift her spirits... briefly. Because the next thing she checked was her bank balance. One invoice was overdue, one had been delayed and the few proposals that were out hadn't been confirmed yet. Feeling the familiar constriction in her chest, she took a deep breath and opened her WhatsApp in search of a distraction from the money anxiety.

A short message from Jordan sat at the top of her chat list.

> Need to talk. The client has asked for some last-minute changes to the pitch. Call when you're free?

Her stomach turned slightly. They were twenty-four hours away from presenting. She, Jordan and Leena had been working for two weeks to shape a pitch that stood out, and it was looking brilliant. They had perfectly fulfilled the client's original request for something fresh and future-focused.

Now it looked like the brief might have changed, meaning their hard work may have mostly gone to waste. Needing to know more, she rang straight away. Jordan answered immediately.

'Hey Soph, heads up, they've just emailed. One of the board members is bringing in another agency they've worked with before. Wants them in the mix for the pitch.'

Sophie frowned. 'So now it's a straight shootout?'

'Pretty much. And they've shifted the goalposts. They're asking everyone to tighten the pitch. Less emphasis on strategy, more on deliverables. They want specifics, packages and clear outcomes.'

A few minutes later, Leena joined the call. Calm, as ever.

'I think we hold the line,' she said. 'They came to us for something different. If we strip it all down now, we just blur into the noise.'

Jordan nodded, but his jaw was tight. 'I get it. But I also get where they're coming from. There's pressure on this board member to prove their guy is the safer choice. If we go too hard on vision, we might lose the room.'

There was silence for a beat.

Then Sophie spoke. 'Then we do what buffalo do. We face it and we say what we believe. But we also show them we've thought through the delivery. Give them something they can say yes to, without losing what makes us different.'

Her voice trembled slightly, but she kept going. 'This is where we lead.'

The tension eased, and the three stayed on the call for forty minutes. Sophie mapped out a simplified three-part structure that was still strategic, but tighter. Leena added tangible examples that the board could picture. Jordan reworked the commercial outline into two clean, confident phases.

There was no scrambling panic to create something that probably wasn't what the client needed. Instead, their energy on the call was calm and confident in what they had to offer.

'This feels right,' Leena said when they'd finished. 'Smart, strong and definitely still us.'

Sophie nodded.

'Yep. Great job, everyone. Now let's put it away, no more edits, and tomorrow, we knock their socks off!'

After the call, Sophie popped out to meet Katie for a quick coffee and some fresh air. The day was fresh but bright, so they opted to sit outside the café with jackets zipped up and enjoy the sunshine.

Sophie walked Katie through yesterday's events with the big pitch. There was a lot at stake for the trio, and getting this project meant a lot, so they were all feeling the pressure. When Sophie mentioned the company name, Katie raised an eyebrow.

'I know one of the board members,' she said.

Sophie blinked. 'Seriously?'

Katie nodded. 'Not, like, really close, but enough to send them a quick message.'

'You'd do that?'

Katie smiled. 'Of course, I can see how hard you've all worked on this. I just want to make sure the right people see it. I can give a quiet endorsement as a name they already trust, telling them to pay attention.'

Sophie let that sink in and felt a feeling of deep gratitude wash over her. She hadn't asked for help, but here she was, once again reminded of the power of showing up and the quiet impact of having the right people in your corner.

•••

Back home, Sophie made a cup of tea and rechecked her inbox. There was one new message:

> Intro from Zara – quick chat?

She opened it.

> Hi Sophie, Zara mentioned you did a great talk at a meeting she was recently at, and said I should speak to you. We're planning a full repositioning later this year, and I'd love to have a quick exploratory call next week if you've got time.

She smiled at the screen and thought, *It's funny how effortless business feels when others are promoting you to the right people.* Then she tapped a reply with her meeting link and grabbed her notebook to write a note:

> Warm leads coming in...
>
> This is the proof.
>
> The right kind of person.
>
> The right conversations.
>
> Momentum is happening!

Early the next morning, Sophie was engrossed in her phone while the kettle boiled, when her daughter came into the kitchen holding a stack of plates and cups from her room. 'You doing that pitch today?'

Sophie nodded. 'Uh-huh, 10am.'

'Is it one of those, like, pick you or pick someone else?'

Sophie looked up from her phone and smiled, before pouring boiling water onto a Yorkshire teabag, ready in her favourite mug.

'Pretty much.'

Her daughter sat on the stool watching her. 'You seem like you believe it this time.'

Sophie looked up. 'Believe what?'

'That you should be the one they pick. You don't look scared this time, you look ready.' Then she surprised Sophie with the perfect analogy: 'It's like when I do try-outs. If I show up just hoping not to mess up, I never do well. But if I believe I belong there, even if I don't get it, I walk away proud.'

Sophie beamed at her teenager's wise words. 'You're being a proper coach today.'

Her daughter grinned. 'And you're being a proper buffalo.'

• • •

Sitting at her desk, stomach full of butterflies, Sophie opened her laptop: fifteen minutes to go.

Her phone buzzed with a voice note from Katie.

> *Quick reminder before you go in: how you show up matters. Not just what you say, but the state you're in when you say it.*
>
> *The best athletes don't roll off the sofa and run their best race. They have a routine. A way to drop into that state where their body and mind are fully present. That applies to business just as much.*
>
> *So take a breath. Sit tall. Shoulders back. Remember who you are. You've done the work. Now just let them see you at your best.*
>
> *You've already earned the room, Sophie. Now go own your square on the screen.*

It was exactly what she needed in that moment. She sat up straight. Planted her feet and rolled her shoulders back, confident, but not stiff. She took a deep centring breath…and clicked 'Join'.

The screen loaded: Jordan, Leena and three board members she didn't yet know. After a few short but warm introductions, it was down to business. Jordan opened.

'We're here to show you how your next phase of growth isn't about more. It's about clearer. And how experience shapes everything your customers believe about you.'

After he talked through his section, Sophie followed, leading with people, rather than visuals.

'Your next clients aren't waiting to be convinced. They're watching to see how you speak, how you present and how easy it is to understand what you do. Clarity creates trust. And trust moves things forward.'

Leena delivered her section and added practical examples, including AI automation to improve onboarding, personalised follow-ups and streamlined communication. The entire pitch was jargon-free and crystal clear on the benefits of their offer.

The board members were curious and asked questions. Then Sophie brought it all together.

'This isn't just a visual rebrand. This is about alignment, both internally and externally, so the experiences your clients have match the high quality of what you deliver.'

There was a pause that felt like it stretched on for hours.

Then one board member said: 'This was… different. We weren't expecting this.'

Another added: 'You've gone way beyond the other pitches. I can see how this would work – you've certainly helped me to see what's possible.'

The chair leaned forwards. 'Three clear experts. One message. You've helped us believe we can actually do this. So, it would appear to be a unanimous yes! Your unique expertise is clear to see, and you've demonstrated your ability to bring all of these elements together to deliver what we need, instead of what we thought we wanted. Thank you for showing us what's possible.'

After a chat about next steps and then goodbyes, Sophie closed the call. She was beyond happy. She had shown up as a leader and encouraged her teammates to stand by what they believed, and it had paid off.

'This calls for a celebratory cup of Yorkshire,' she said to the empty room, and headed to the kitchen with a definite spring in her step.

Action steps: Lead with purpose, not pressure

You don't grow a meaningful business by doing everything yourself. You grow it by leading intentionally, creating real alignment and showing up when it matters. Prepared, steady and supported. This chapter focuses on building the internal state and external structure that help you lead when the pressure builds. Techniques to support you include:

1. Anchor yourself before big moments

What helps you show up as your best self? Write a short list of three things you can do in the five to ten minutes before an important meeting, pitch or conversation.

Examples are:

- Sit up straight, breathe deeply and read a sentence from your 'why'.
- Review your client notes and remember what matters to your clients.
- Picture someone you've already helped and recall the impact.

This is your pre-performance routine. Make it a habit.

2. Identify your inner circle of support

Write down three people who:

- Believe in what you do
- Would speak up for you if you asked
- Help you think clearly under pressure

Then write your answer to the question: 'How can I involve or lean on them more?' This might be for feedback, encouragement, a recommendation or just a reality check.

3. Redefine what a win looks like

List the moments that showed you're heading in the right direction, even if they weren't final outcomes. For example:

- A great conversation
- A warm referral
- Someone asking how to introduce you
- Feeling confident in a proposal

Momentum often shows up as small signs you're on the right track. Start to notice them and bring more small wins into your awareness.

4. Lead like a team, not as a solo act

Ask yourself:

- Where am I still trying to do everything myself?
- How can I bring someone in, even lightly, to strengthen what I offer?

Whether it's co-creating, subcontracting or collaboration, find one way to stop positioning yourself as a one-person solution. Clients feel safer when they see a team, even if it's part-time, project-based or behind the scenes.

BUFFALO REMINDER

When the pressure builds, lead with purpose, not panic.

Anchor yourself. Build support. Step in with clarity.

You don't have to carry it alone to own the room.

To access extra resources, scan the QR code below, or go to www.bemorebuffalo.com.

NINE

The Buffalo Way

It had been three days since the pitch. Sophie still hadn't fully processed the response they'd had. A resounding yes right after the pitch! It was unheard of. The board's words echoed in her head: *Three clear experts. One message. You've helped us believe we can actually do this.*

The paperwork was in progress, contracts were being drawn up, and project timelines had been agreed. Leena had looped in her legal contact, and Jordan was coordinating a smooth onboarding for their new client.

A lot was happening, yet the biggest change wasn't this new collaboration. It was *in* Sophie – her mindset, actions, habits and behaviours.

Just a few weeks ago, she'd been stuck in desperation, worry and stress, the weight of carrying it all alone becoming too much. Yet now, only a short time later, the difference was mind-blowing. Something had clicked, and now she felt calm and centred. She wasn't chasing anymore, just moving steadily towards a clear goal.

• • •

Monday morning started as it usually did, with a hot cup of tea and her laptop open before the kids were fully awake. Sophie flicked through her notes, scrolled through messages and opened her diary. She had various calls booked in: a check-in with Natalie, a chat with a potential new collaborator, even a follow-up from someone she'd introduced weeks ago, thanking her and asking how they could help her now.

She sat still for a moment and let it all sink in.

This was all down to Katie sharing the *Be More Buffalo* book with her and then checking in with some guidance and accountability, too.

But then, she mused, maybe she deserved some credit, too. After all, she could have just read the book without doing any of the tasks. If she was honest, it was using the notebook, getting honest with herself and doing the tasks that had really driven the change.

Katie messaged later that day:

> You've come a long way in a short space of time. But the reason it stuck is because you didn't just change what you did. You changed how you showed up.

That was it.

Being more buffalo wasn't about bullish bravado or mindset tricks. It wasn't even a productivity hack. It was about how she faced things. About not running from the tricky or uncomfortable things – or from herself. It was showing up for the hard parts instead of avoiding them. Starting the conversation. Asking for help. Making the introduction. Following through.

It was about doing this all with others, instead of alone.

•••

Twelve months on, the ripple effect was plain to see.

The project that had begun with a bold pitch? It had grown massively. What started as a brand refresh had turned into a wider customer experience initiative, then into ongoing strategy retainers, which led to referrals, one of which had led to a collaboration with a national organisation she would never have approached on her own.

The trio hadn't just delivered the project; they had become an integral part of the client's future, and that had changed everything. The success with that client had done more than pay the bills. It had shifted Sophie's positioning. Her confidence. Her work. Her referrals.

It wasn't all plain sailing – there were delays, curveballs and times when she felt stretched again – but she didn't spiral into overwhelm or panic like before. She held steady, faced the storms and found her way through.

She was building her business differently now, and the thing that surprised her most was how good it felt to face the things she'd previously spent so long avoiding.

Those quiet coffee chats she'd booked with Rani, Tom and others? They'd all developed into the perfect support system for her and the business. Rani now managed her calendar and client comms, which had freed up more time and headspace than she'd ever imagined it would. Tom had created a simple project-flow system that now kept her on track and working efficiently, which, again, freed up more time. She'd brought in a strategist part-time to help shape proposals and lead early conversations, and she was loving having someone else to bounce ideas around with.

Sophie still led the way and did the design work, she just wasn't doing everything alone. Each task she signed off gave her more space to lead and grow the business – not just bigger, but stronger, more structured and sustainable. She was no longer a freelancer; she was finally a business owner.

•••

The cottage was cosy, welcoming and so peaceful. Comfy sofas with soft cushions and warm blankets sat waiting to envelop you in front of an open fire. Logs crackled in the fireplace, and a pot of tea sat steeping in the kitchen. Sophie had booked the weekend months ago. Not for business, but as a thank you.

Katie had arrived the night before, a broad smile spreading across her face as she took in her home for the weekend. Now they sat on the terrace, wrapped in blankets and watching clouds roll behind the hills.

Katie looked out, then turned to Sophie. 'You booked the Cotswolds. How did you know I'd always wanted to come here?'

'You told me months ago. One of those early conversations when we were talking about what we wanted from the year.'

Katie's eyes crinkled. 'You listened.'

Sophie nodded. 'You taught me how.'

They sat in quiet for a while.

Then Sophie spoke.

'There's someone I've been helping. A coach. She's talented, but she's hit a wall. I've been doing what you did with me. I gave her the book and a new notebook, and then I've been checking in, one step at a time.'

Katie grinned. 'And just like that, another buffalo joins the herd.'

Back inside, the friends were sitting sipping tea and chatting by the warmth of the fire, when Katie's phone rang. She glanced at it. 'Oh, it's Dan.' She answered, then looked across at Sophie. 'I'm actually with her right now, hold on, I'll pass you over.'

Sophie took the phone. 'Hi?'

'Sophie, it's Dan. I've heard about your journey this year and how you've helped others, too. I'd love to invite you to speak at one of our upcoming conferences. Just to share your story, no pressure. Just you, as you are.'

Sophie paused. She could feel the nerves, but she didn't shrink.

'Yes. I'd be honoured.'

Dan replied without hesitation. 'Brilliant, let's arrange a catch-up next week.'

After dinner, they opened a bottle of red that Sophie had been saving, but it wasn't to celebrate the success of the past year or the invite to take the stage at the conference. It was to mark what came next.

They sat at the big oak table together, notebooks open and pens ready. This time, it wasn't to reflect, it was to plan. A bigger future, built on clarity, connection and courage.

They weren't avoiding storms. They were walking into them. Together.

Action steps: The buffalo way

This final chapter isn't about wrapping things up. It's about realising that growth is not a finish line. It's a way of life. A way of showing up, building together and staying connected. These steps will help you keep that rhythm going.

1. Mark your progress with a quiet win

Look back over the past few months. What has changed in how you show up, think, connect or lead?

Pick one example and write it down. It could be a referral that came from nowhere, a project that felt easier or a moment you handled with more clarity.

Momentum builds when we notice how far we have come.

2. Revisit your F Network™

Check in with your Five, your Fifteen and your Fifty. Who needs to move inwards? Who hasn't heard from you in a while?

Send two messages this week:

- One to someone you want to deepen your connection with
- One to someone you want to thank for being part of your progress

Stay consistent. That's where the strength is.

3. Build before you're busy

Revisit your list of potential team members from Chapter Seven. Is what you wrote down still relevant now?

List the tasks or decisions that often slow you down when work gets busy. Then ask:

- Who could help with this?
- What process would make this easier next time?

You don't need to hire right away, but you can start a conversation or block time to build a simple system.

4. Choose someone to help

Think of someone who is earlier on the journey than you – someone who might benefit from a check-in, a small nudge or a quick conversation.

Send them a message. Just like Katie did for Sophie. You could even send them a copy of this book and a notebook. One notebook. One step. One new buffalo.

You don't have to wait for clarity. Or confidence. Or permission.

You just need to move.

Face the storm. Build the herd.

Keep showing up, together.

To access extra resources, scan the QR code below, or go to www.bemorebuffalo.com.

Epilogue

Keep facing forward.

The herd doesn't run from the storm. It turns into it. Together.

That's what Sophie learned. Not in a workshop, podcast or passive activity, but from walking through the storm herself – step by step, breath by breath, one brave reflection, decision and conversation at a time.

There was no perfect moment, no sudden breakthrough. Just small decisions followed through. The kind that build trust and shift identity. The kind that leave you changed.

Sophie didn't learn to outrun fear. She learned to face it with support beside her.

She didn't wait for confidence to arrive. She acted anyway, built habits, made space and asked for help.

She didn't chase a business breakthrough. She built relationships that brought it to her.

As the months unfolded, she began to understand something deeper.

Being more buffalo had never been about being brave for the sake of it. It was about thinking differently. Connecting differently. Living differently. With clarity. With courage. And with people who would walk beside her, not just clap from the sidelines.

When the storms come, and they always do, it isn't the solo runners who get through best. It's the ones who stop waiting. Who face forward. And who do it together.

Bonus preview from the upcoming book: Friendship Fuels Business™

The room was still.

Not the kind of quiet that comes from manners or expectation – the kind that comes from presence. From people who were intently listening.

Sophie stood centre stage, one hand resting lightly on the lectern, the other relaxed and open as she spoke. 'We talk a lot about visibility in business. About strategy, scaling and systems. But what no one told me at the start was how lonely it would feel.'

She glanced at the third row, and Katie's warm smile anchored her for a moment. Then she looked around the room at the sea of faces, all seemingly hanging on her every word.

'I thought I needed tactics. And yes, I did. But what I needed first...was people.'

She let her words hang in the air, allowing them to sink in as the pause stretched out for a moment.

'The right people changed everything. They didn't rescue me. They reminded me who I was. They challenged me. Believed in me. Walked with me when I was struggling to do it all alone.'

She reached for her notebook, well used and carried everywhere, edges worn – the same one Katie had slid across that café table all those months ago. She held it up.

'This notebook started with a question. One that helped me face the storm I'd been trying to outrun. That question was simply...what are you avoiding?'

Emotion welled up in her; eyes prickling, she smiled. Not for effect, but from realising just how far she had come.

She continued with her keynote until she came to her closing statement.

'And now? I'm building a business rooted in something deeper than goals. I'm building it on this...'

She paused, took a breath and clicked to the last slide.

'Friendship Fuels Business.'

Silence again.

The message landed with everyone in the room. You could see it in the stillness, the nodding heads, the people leaning forwards, enthralled, and the quiet exhalation of someone who felt seen. Because they understood.

This wasn't Sophie's closing chapter. It was her next beginning.

Action Steps Summary

Chapter One: Spot the storm

This chapter is about recognition. About naming what you've been carrying and admitting when something needs to change. Use the steps below to help you identify areas for development.

1. Write it down

What storm have you been avoiding facing? It might be a money issue, a lack of direction or something more personal. Get specific.

2. Ask yourself

Reflect on these questions:

- What is this costing me, emotionally or financially, to avoid?
- What would change if I stopped dodging it?

3. Make one decision

It doesn't need to fix everything; just make it clear. For example, a commitment to speak up, change your offer or start something that's yours.

4. Start your notebook

Keep it beside you as you read this book. Use it to capture your reflections, decisions and progress.

5. Say it out loud or share it with someone

Naming your storm out loud makes it more real. Share it with a trusted friend or mentor. You don't need to go it alone.

BUFFALO REMINDER

You can't move forward if you won't face what's in front of you.

The longer you avoid the storm, the longer it controls you.

Name it. Map it. Take one step.

The buffalo don't wait for perfect conditions. They face it together. So can you.

Chapter Two: Overcome fear and procrastination

This chapter is about turning awareness into movement. Not big leaps, just intentional small steps in the right direction. Use the prompts below to move through fear instead of waiting for it to disappear.

1. Name the fear clearly

Choose one thing you've been avoiding in your business. Write it at the top of the page. Keep it simple and specific.

Examples could include: 'Raising my rates', 'Launching a new offer', 'Saying no to a draining client'.

2. Use the Best/Worst/Most Likely tool

Draw three columns as below and answer the questions about the thing you wrote at the top of the page.

Best Case	**Worst Case**	**Most Likely**
What's the ideal outcome?	What's the realistic worst-case scenario?	What is most probable?

You'll often realise the worst isn't as bad as it felt.

3. Create a fear/action list

Draw two columns and give them the following headings:

- What I'm Afraid Of
- What I Can Do Anyway

Then, jot down your answers. Examples could include:

- If I promote myself, I'll come across as too confident.
- Post something useful or honest.

4. Take one step

Pick one action from your list of things you can do anyway, and do it today. The list might include:

- Send the message.
- Say no.
- Ask.
- Begin.

Then write down what happened – not just the result, but how it felt.

BUFFALO REMINDER

Fear will show up. That means you're moving out of your comfort zone.

Don't wait until you feel ready.

Start small.

Even the smallest action cuts through anxiety more than overthinking ever will.

Chapter Three: Build resilience

This chapter is about building resilience in the face of adversity and challenges. Use these tools to recover from setbacks with clarity instead of collapse.

1. Try the PODA reset

When something knocks you off track, write this in your notebook:

- **Pause** – What just happened? Let yourself feel it.
- **Observe** – What are the facts? What did you learn?
- **Decide** – What now? What matters most?
- **Act** – What's one small thing you can do to move forward?

2. Create your Go for No list

Draw three columns and give them the following headings:

- People to Follow Up With
- People to Meet for a Conversation
- People to Collaborate With

Jot down a few people below each heading. Reach out to them and track the responses you receive: the noes and the yeses. Let both move you forward.

3. Prioritise your own business

Treat your brand like a client project. Define your message. Shape your identity. Speak up. No more hiding behind the work.

Resilience isn't about pushing through without feeling.

It's about moving again after the hit.

Keep showing up. Keep walking forward.

The storm is part of it – but so is your strength.

Chapter Four: Create clear goals and small wins

This chapter is about replacing vague ambition with focused movement. Don't just hope progress will happen. Make it visible. Make it practical. Make it yours. Use the following steps to help you work towards this.

1. Use the CLEAR framework for goal setting

C – Clearly define the outcome

L – Link it to your purpose

E – Establish milestones

A – Create action steps for this week

R – Review and adjust weekly

2. Focus on small wins

Write one simple task per day that moves your bigger goal forward. Complete it before anything else.

3. Build your weekly momentum list

At the start of the week, write the answers to these questions:

- What do I want to happen next?
- What actions can I take this week to move towards taking them?

Review and tick off as you go.

4. Reach out to someone

Check in with someone in your network with no agenda – just a genuine 'How are you?'

5. Collaborate on a next step

Don't do it all alone. Pick one goal you've been stuck on and ask: 'Who could help me move this forward?'

BUFFALO REMINDER

Small wins are far from small. Each one is a sign of movement, direction and progress. Build them daily, and the big wins will follow.

Chapter Five: Build relationships that grow your business

You already know more people than you think. The goal isn't to collect contacts, it's to connect with intention and then deepen those relationships. This chapter is about seeing your network more clearly, and tending to it with purpose, not pressure. Below are some ideas to help you do this.

1. Map your F Network™

Draw three concentric circles on a blank page. Label them:

- **The Five** – People who know what you're building and speak to you regularly
- **The Fifteen** – People who respect your work but don't hear from you often
- **The Fifty** – Friendly connections and acquaintances

Now list real names in each circle. Start with who comes to mind, and aim for at least three in each category. Don't force it, this is a working list, not a test.

2. Start a weekly relationship rhythm

Set a gentle, repeatable cadence for yourself. For example:

- **Each week**: Check in with two people from your Five.
- **Each fortnight**: Reconnect with one person from your Fifteen.
- **Each month**: Reach out meaningfully to someone in your Fifty.
- **Bonus**: Make one helpful introduction or share something valuable.

You can block time out in your calendar for this or set reminders, but remember: this isn't about doing it on autopilot or as a copy-and-paste task. It needs to be genuine and considered, something you *feel*, not just something you *do*.

3. Pay it forward this week

Look back through recent notes from conversations, events or posts. Who mentioned a challenge or goal? Offer something small but thoughtful: a useful article, a kind check-in or an introduction that might help.

Reach out to one person this week without expecting anything back. For example:

> Hey, I was thinking of you, I know someone who might be able to help. Would you like an intro?

These small gestures often mean more than you realise.

4. Ask yourself the PLU question

Review your current clients, collaborators and the people you spend time with. For each one, ask yourself: 'Is this person PLU?' People Like Us are those who value your work, get your style and energise rather than drain you.

If they aren't, that's OK. Not everyone will be the right fit. You don't need to chase people who drain you or try to convince the wrong ones to stay. Sometimes gaining clarity means letting some things go so you can make space for better things to come through, even when it comes to people.

BUFFALO REMINDER

Real relationships are built over time, not through transactions.

Storms are easier to face when you have people alongside you.

Keep showing up and making time and space for meaningful connection to take root.

Your network isn't just who you know, it's who you're building with.

Chapter Six: Create a clear offer and invite opportunities

Being brilliant at what you do isn't enough. People need to understand it, and know how to talk about it when you're not in the room. This chapter is about getting clear on your offer, making it memorable and setting yourself up to receive referrals and invitations, and have conversations that count. Use these steps to help you.

1. Write the first clear version of your offer

On a blank page, answer these prompts as simply as possible:

- Who do you help? (Be specific. Name their stage, mindset or situation.)
- What do you help them with? (Focus on outcomes, not just deliverables.)
- Why does it matter? (What changes for them?)

Now shape it into one sentence that starts: 'I help…'. Remember, it doesn't need to be perfect on the first try, just honest and clear enough to test out.

2. Say it out loud

Share your new offer in one live conversation this week. It could be at a networking meeting, a coffee catch-up or even during a quick Zoom with a close business friend.

Pay attention to how it feels when you say it, and how people respond. Clarity gets noticed and remembered.

3. Make a 'referral-ready' follow-up message

Write a short message someone could use to introduce you. Include:

- Who you work with
- The kind of challenge you help solve
- A friendly link to a short call or contact page

An example might be:

> Sophie helps growing businesses that feel like they've outgrown their brand. She helps them define who they are and show up clearly as they grow. If that sounds useful, let me know and I can send you a link to book a call with her.

Save this. It will make it easier for people to refer you.

4. Ask for feedback from two to three trusted people

Pick people who will be honest. Send them your draft offer and ask:

- Does this sound like me?
- Is it clear who I work with and what I do?
- Can you think of someone who might need this?

Use the bits that land; don't do a complete U-turn, just make minor tweaks and refine gradually.

BUFFALO REMINDER

People can't send you opportunities if they don't understand what you do.

Say it clearly. Say it often. Say it in places where the right people are listening.

Chapter Seven: Strengthen your systems to scale what works

Momentum without structure creates stress. This chapter is your invitation to slow down – not to stop, but to stabilise. Strong systems and the right support help you scale without losing yourself in the process. Take the following five steps to help you achieve this.

1. Spot the strain

Write down three signs that you're hitting your limit. It might be:

- Forgetting follow-ups
- Losing track of proposals or projects
- Feeling like you can't respond properly to new opportunities

Name them. Then underline the one you've felt most this week. Awareness is the first step.

2. List your support gaps

Look at your week honestly. What are you still doing yourself that someone else could help with?

Common areas to consider are:

- Scheduling
- Proposal creation or formatting
- Inbox sorting or client comms
- Social media admin

- Follow-up or onboarding steps
- Content repurposing

Pick one area and commit to starting a conversation about it. You don't have to hire, just explore.

3. Map your virtual team

On a Page or Doc, create three columns with the following headings:

- What I Need Help With
- People I Know Who Could Help
- Next Step (Message, Research or Referral)

Think of people you've met at events, in groups or through mutual contacts and jot them down. Start with those you trust or want to learn more about.

4. Book one call this week

Reach out to someone you're considering for part of your virtual team. Use a no-pressure message. For example:

> Hey, I'm starting to look ahead and think about getting support in place as things grow. Would love a quick chat to understand what you offer and how it works.

You're not committing to anything, but it's the start of turning a job into a business.

5. Recognise the room you're already in

Take five minutes to reflect on the following questions:

- Who are the people supporting you already, through advice, introductions, encouragement or collaboration?
- What groups or events have felt energising, not draining?
- Where do you feel like you can be yourself?

Write your answers down.

You might not need to join something new; you might just need to show up more intentionally where you already are.

Don't wait until you're overwhelmed to build structure.

Strong systems are the foundation, not the reward.

Support doesn't slow you down, it lets you go further. Together.

Chapter Eight: Lead with purpose, not pressure

You don't grow a meaningful business by doing everything yourself. You grow it by leading intentionally, creating real alignment and showing up when it matters. Prepared, steady and supported. This chapter focuses on building the internal state and external structure that help you lead when the pressure builds. Techniques to support you include:

1. Anchor yourself before big moments

What helps you show up as your best self? Write a short list of three things you can do in the five to ten minutes before an important meeting, pitch or conversation.

Examples are:

- Sit up straight, breathe deeply and read a sentence from your 'why'.
- Review your client notes and remember what matters to your clients.
- Picture someone you've already helped and recall the impact.

This is your pre-performance routine. Make it a habit.

2. Identify your inner circle of support

Write down three people who:

- Believe in what you do
- Would speak up for you if you asked
- Help you think clearly under pressure

Then write your answer to the question: 'How can I involve or lean on them more?' This might be for feedback, encouragement, a recommendation or just a reality check.

3. Redefine what a win looks like

List the moments that showed you're heading in the right direction, even if they weren't final outcomes. For example:

- A great conversation
- A warm referral
- Someone asking how to introduce you
- Feeling confident in a proposal

Momentum often shows up as small signs you're on the right track. Start to notice them and bring more small wins into your awareness.

4. Lead like a team, not as a solo act

Ask yourself:

- Where am I still trying to do everything myself?
- How can I bring someone in, even lightly, to strengthen what I offer?

Whether it's co-creating, subcontracting or collaboration, find one way to stop positioning yourself as a one-person solution. Clients feel safer when they see a team, even if it's part-time, project-based or behind the scenes.

BUFFALO REMINDER

When the pressure builds, lead with purpose, not panic.

Anchor yourself. Build support. Step in with clarity.

You don't have to carry it alone to own the room.

Chapter Nine: The buffalo way

This final chapter isn't about wrapping things up. It's about realising that growth is not a finish line. It's a way of life. A way of showing up, building together and staying connected. These steps will help you keep that rhythm going.

1. Mark your progress with a quiet win

Look back over the past few months. What has changed in how you show up, think, connect or lead?

Pick one example and write it down. It could be a referral that came from nowhere, a project that felt easier or a moment you handled with more clarity.

Momentum builds when we notice how far we have come.

2. Revisit your F Network™

Check in with your Five, your Fifteen and your Fifty. Who needs to move inwards? Who hasn't heard from you in a while?

Send two messages this week:

- One to someone you want to deepen your connection with
- One to someone you want to thank for being part of your progress

Stay consistent. That's where the strength is.

3. Build before you're busy

Revisit your list of potential team members from Chapter Seven. Is what you wrote down still relevant now?

List the tasks or decisions that often slow you down when work gets busy. Then ask:

- Who could help with this?
- What process would make this easier next time?

You don't need to hire right away, but you can start a conversation or block time to build a simple system.

4. Choose someone to help

Think of someone who is earlier on the journey than you – someone who might benefit from a check-in, a small nudge or a quick conversation.

Send them a message. Just like Katie did for Sophie. You could even send them a copy of this book and a notebook. One notebook. One step. One new buffalo.

BUFFALO REMINDER

You don't have to wait for clarity. Or confidence. Or permission.

You just need to move.

Face the storm. Build the herd.

Keep showing up, together.

Acknowledgements

First, thank you to Lou, my partner in everything. Your support, encouragement and belief in me have made this book possible in more ways than you know.

To Greg Middleton, thank you for sparking the idea that became Circle Networks. That early phone conversation back in 2020 planted a seed that has grown into something that is changing lives around the world.

To Gillian Schofield, co-author and editor, thank you for turning my messy first draft into a book we're proud of. You helped bring structure and clarity to every chapter.

To Elliot Kay, thank you for helping me shape the original *Be More Buffalo* talk. That early work laid the foundation for everything that followed. Thank you for introducing me to Joe Gregory to help publish the book with Rethink Press.

To Ailsa Stinson, thank you for your strategic thinking and accountability in developing the brand strategy that helped shape the message and the movement behind this book.

To Frank Stebbing, thank you for the creative work that brought the brand to life through your design expertise.

Thank you to Chris Griffiths, Paul McGowan and Mel Foley, you probably didn't realise it at the time, but your mindset, your energy and the way you showed up in business helped shape what *Be More Buffalo* stands for. This book carries a lot of your early influence.

Thank you to authors and friends who have had a huge impact: Andrea Waltz and Richard Fenton, authors of *Go For No*, and Bob Burg and John David Mann, whose book *The Go Giver* inspired the core fundamentals of Circle Networks in helping others first.

To Ann Owen: without you knowing it, you shared PLU – People Like Us – with Ailsa, and I knew it was a value we needed in our community. Thank you.

Thank you to everyone in the Circle Networks community who lives these ideas daily. This book was written with you, for you and because of people like us.

The Author

Jamie Stewart is the founder of Circle Networks, a global community built on the belief that *Friendship Fuels Business*™. After helping thousands of business owners grow through meaningful connections, he wrote this book to share the mindset and framework that changed everything.

www.bemorebuffalo.com

www.circlenetworks.co.uk

Gillian Schofield is the founder of Kustom Copy, where she helps small businesses sound more human and a lot less boring. A copywriter, strategist, and champion of ethical marketing, she believes connection beats perfection every time.

🌐 www.kustomcopy.co.uk